This isn't a book with information and steps in it. It's a book about the power of love to set us free. Danielle doesn't just talk about this in books; she lives it out on the streets. This book won't make you want to be like Danielle—it will make you want to be like Jesus.

BOB GOFF
New York Times bestselling author of *Love Does*

If you're searching and longing for freedom in your life, find someone who knows what it feels like to be free, and lives it. Find someone who understands that freedom is not a cheap quick fix and that it's often hard, sacrificial, and disciplined. Find someone who's failed and gotten up again, with skin in the game and scars to prove it. Someone who is compassionate enough to love you where you're at but challenging enough to not let you stay there. Find someone who can't stop working toward setting people free because she has discovered the kind of good news too good not to share. Danielle offers us all this and more in *The Ultimate Exodus*.

Get the book, and get back on your journey—to freedom.

JO SAXTON
Cohost of *Lead Stories Podcast* and board chair of 3D Movements

In *The Ultimate Exodus*, Danielle Strickland reminds us that God invades our ordinary, everyday lives in ways that lead us closer to true freedom. She knows this, of course, because she's experienced that liberty in real ways most of

us can only imagine. As she retells some of the ways God has led her from the edge to an exodus, we are reminded again that life is more than just one Red Sea crossing.

REGGIE JOINER
Founder and CEO of Orange

The Ultimate Exodus effervesces with Danielle Strickland's characteristic passion, compassion, and clarity. It addresses some of the most pressing, pervasive, and personal issues of our time, unlocking freedom and greater joy for us all.

PETE GREIG
Bestselling author, pastor, and founder of 24-7 Prayer

This is a book about getting free and becoming a real and an honest-to-goodness follower of God—disciplined, focused, evangelizing, praying, serving, sabbathing, giving, and believing. And because I know Danielle Strickland, I can say that it's also written by one. You simply must read it.

MICHAEL FROST
Author of *Surprise the World*

Danielle Strickland gives off the fragrance of Jesus. And in *The Ultimate Exodus*, she reminds us that Jesus came not just to make bad people good but to set oppressed people free and bring dead people back to life. It's a beautiful book.

SHANE CLAIBORNE
Author, activist, "red-letter" Christian, and recovering sinner

It's common to find a book that would be good for someone you know. It's rare to find a book that would be good for *everyone* you know. Simple, beautiful, and comprehensive, *The Ultimate Exodus* holds treasures of Danielle's life experiences, and the depth of her spiritual reflections is poetic and life changing. While *freedom* can be a buzzword, this journey through the central metaphor of Scripture is not only hopeful but also enlightening and deeply enthralling. Through *The Ultimate Exodus*, you will catch a glimpse of the beauty of God's love for his children and gain invaluable perspective on how to attain the freedom promised in Christ. This book is a gem.

KEN WYTSMA
Pastor, educator, and author of *The Grand Paradox* and *Create vs. Copy*

I'm a total Danielle Strickland fan. Not only is she one of the most outstanding speakers around today, but she's also a radical witness to Jesus and a good writer to boot. Danielle speaks with the authority of someone who lives out her message in the rough-and-tumble of life.

ALAN HIRSCH
Award-winning author on missional Christianity and leadership

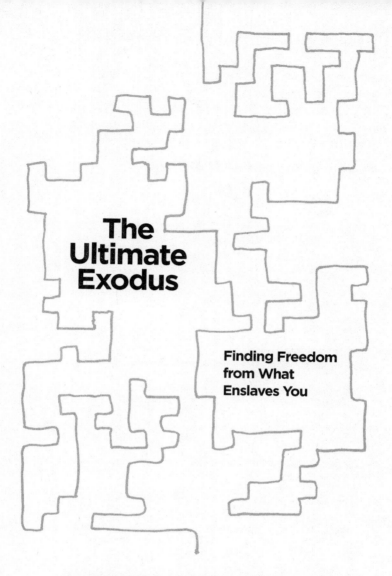

The Ultimate Exodus

Finding Freedom from What Enslaves You

DANIELLE STRICKLAND

A NavPress resource published in alliance
with Tyndale House Publishers, Inc.

NavPress is the publishing ministry of The Navigators, an international Christian organization and leader in personal spiritual development. NavPress is committed to helping people grow spiritually and enjoy lives of meaning and hope through personal and group resources that are biblically rooted, culturally relevant, and highly practical.

For more information, visit www.NavPress.com.

The Ultimate Exodus: Finding Freedom from What Enslaves You

Copyright © 2017 by The Salvation Army. All rights reserved.

A NavPress resource published in alliance with Tyndale House Publishers, Inc.

NAVPRESS and the NAVPRESS logo are registered trademarks of NavPress, The Navigators, Colorado Springs, CO. *TYNDALE* is a registered trademark of Tyndale House Publishers, Inc. Absence of ® in connection with marks of NavPress or other parties does not indicate an absence of registration of those marks.

The Team:
Don Pape, Publisher
David Zimmerman, Acquisitions Editor
Jennifer Phelps, Designer

Cover illustration of maze copyright © printcolorfun.com. Used with permission. All rights reserved.

Some of the anecdotal illustrations in this book are true to life and are included with the permission of the persons involved. All other illustrations are composites of real situations, and any resemblance to people living or dead is purely coincidental.

For information about special discounts for bulk purchases, please contact Tyndale House Publishers at csresponse@tyndale.com or call 800-323-9400.

Cataloging-in-Publication Data is available.

ISBN 978-1-63146-647-2

Printed in the United States of America

23 22 21 20 19
7   6   5   4

To Jan, who faithfully unravels oppression with cupcakes.

To Stepfanie, because flowers are meant to bloom.

To Taanis, who demonstrates that freedom is never too hard and never too late with God.

To those who are trapped in modern-day slavery. We hear your cries.

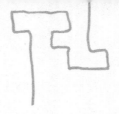

Contents

Introduction

I WAS INCREDIBLY privileged to visit Haiti recently. I traveled there with Compassion International to meet up with my sponsor child and his mother. It was impacting in every way. You can imagine the mix of pain and joy as I heard the story of extreme poverty and its devastating consequences in the lives of this family I had become entwined with. I also celebrated the hope of a different future for a few of them through the faithfulness and strength of a local church offering a lifeline of resources. Hope and hardship work like this—almost in tandem with each other. Great celebration gives way to desperate feelings of powerlessness, and then back again to celebration. Like a great pendulum of the heart.

One of the things I was particularly interested in as I visited Haiti was its complex history of slavery and freedom. Haiti is the first black republic on the face of the earth. Seven hundred thousand Africans were taken and enslaved on this French colony in the seventeenth and eighteenth centuries. They worked the plantations there to keep the most profitable colony in history working smoothly—until one person got an idea, an idea that would change the world.

Of course it's more complicated than that, but at the same time, it's as simple as that: Someone in Haiti had the idea that these enslaved Africans weren't born to be slaves.

Just think about that for a minute. It is what we call a revolutionary idea.

Over a bit of time and talking and dreaming and plotting, some hard, cold statistics came to light, chief among them that slaves in Haiti outnumbered the slavers—by a *lot*. A revolution began, and it was bloody. Most historians agree it was one of the bloodiest revolutions in history. The French masters were roundly defeated, and the African slaves were now free. Well, kind of.

After an incredible uprising and a declaration of freedom for the people of Haiti, there began a complex and meandering story of exploitation and political unrest. Waves of injustice from without and within made the Haiti I eventually visited oppressed by slavery of many different flavors. Gone were the plantations, but still present was the poverty. Gone were the shackles and chains, but still present was systemic political corruption that kept people living in constant fear. Gone were the old colonial "masters," but still present was the fastest growing crime in Haiti—child slavery. Former slaves were now slavers themselves. What happened?

What happened is what always happens, it seems: The same story is repeated in history over and over again. Slavery always returns. Oppression finds new forms, and people become entangled in its web. To be liberated from slavery, it turns out, we must confront not just external realities but internal ones.

I was visiting a friend of mine who for years has been working with the poorest folks in Asia. She routinely sees women exiting the slavery that is the sex industry. I asked her about one particular woman I had met with that morning: "How long has she been free?"

My friend wisely answered, "She's been out of the brothel for six months, but she's still on the journey of freedom." It takes only a few moments, my friend told me, for a woman to be freed from the room where she is held as a sex slave. But it can take many years to get the sex slavery out of the woman.

Freedom is a long-term work, and it often comes only from the inside out.

A little verse in the New Testament, Galatians 5:1, spells it out quite well: "It is for freedom that Christ has set us free. Stand firm, then, and do not let yourselves be burdened again by a yoke of slavery" (NIV). In other words, Jesus has created a way for us to experience freedom. Outside and in. Be free, and don't be slaves again.

The warning Paul offers the Galatians is exceptionally prophetic. Slavery always returns, but it may return in different forms. Oppression has a thousand different colors. In the case of the Galatian church, the people were beginning to use religion itself as a form of slavery—and you don't have to be around very long on this earth to know that religion can be a harsh slave master. But then again, anything can be oppressive. Coffee can have the fresh taste of a morning pick-me-up, but a tragic story of capitalistic greed and blood may be woven into its blend. Wealth can be freeing, but the inner lives of many extremely wealthy people show signs of despair and destruction. So what is with this combo punch? Things that set free and oppress? Can slavery ever end? Can freedom ever come?

This book says yes. Slavery may always return, but freedom is bound to come. I'm an eternal optimist. I believe that freedom is every human being's birthright. By an eternal intention and a supernatural power, we were born to be free. God made us that way. It's the oldest origin story on earth: humanity made to be free.

Yet a story of slavery runs through the heart of each of us. Brokenness is the human condition, and in fact we tend to lean into oppression. Even the Bible warns us that once we are set free, we have to be on guard to avoid letting slavery back in.

That's some amazing advice. But how? How can we truly be set free—and then stay free? What does it look like to enter into a new way of living, a life free from oppression?

Thankfully there is a story that helps us with these questions. It's *the* story of freedom—the grand story of God's people, caught in oppression and needing to get free, and of God unleashing a course of events that sets them free and establishes them as a new nation under his leadership.

This story is not of the Disney variety. It's harsh and

truthful, full of the frustrations and realities of fighting for freedom in the midst of external and internal oppression. But to learn the freedom story of the people of God is to find the keys to our own freedom—the ultimate exodus, into freedom, from the inside out.

I pray you'll find some keys that unlock freedom for your life as you read this book.

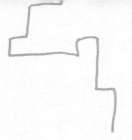

The Exodus

A Quick Review

JUST TO BE SURE we are all on the same page, let's clarify what's meant by the story of the Exodus.

Exodus is a book in the Bible. In that book are the main elements of a larger story, extending through multiple Bible books, of God's people getting free from oppression. I recommend you read it.

The Exodus story includes the story of Moses, which has been the subject of many Hollywood productions. So if you'd rather watch a movie, there are a bunch to choose from. My kids like the animated film *The Prince of Egypt*. DreamWorks Pictures produced it. It has great music and tells the tale in ninety minutes—which, although entertaining and very moving, means it is not exactly accurate.

Speaking of inaccurate, *The Ten Commandments* is an oldie but a goodie. It stars Charlton Heston as Moses. Or, if you like it fresh, *Exodus: Gods and Kings* is a newer rendition, with Christian Bale in the lead role.

I shouldn't be too critical of these movie treatments, of

course, as this book itself is only scratching the surface of some potential lessons we can learn on our own way out of oppression. *Exodus* means "a going out"; the Exodus story has "exit" signs lit up all over the place. You can't miss them once I've pointed them out. The reason they are lit up is the same reason Exodus made it into the Bible: It's important to know the way out when you need it.

The story line of the Exodus is shared by individuals and a community. This shouldn't surprise us. After all, our lives are all connected. The Exodus story starts not in the book of Exodus but in the book of Genesis, the first book of the Bible—the best stories are always too complicated to fit into one book—when Joseph is sold into slavery by his jealous brothers. (To be fair to them, he seemed to be a bit of a pain.) Through an incredibly twisted story line, Joseph ends up second in command of Egypt, and because God speaks to him in dreams, he saves Egypt from famine and prospers Egypt's economy. His whole family (the small beginnings of Israel—the people of God) is saved with Egypt.

Egypt's Pharaoh invites Joseph's family to live in Egypt (and benefit from the food that Joseph has managed to save). He gives them the land of Goshen—the finest land in all of Egypt for shepherding. Three hundred years later (that's where the story picks up in the book of Exodus), a new Pharaoh doesn't know Joseph or the story of the Israelites in Egypt. This Pharaoh feels threatened by the Israelites (ignorance is dangerous) because they have been blessed like rabbits and have kept multiplying over the centuries. Instead of seeing them as successful friends, this Pharaoh views the Israelites as a potential enemy and begins to oppress them, making their lives hard with work and ordering midwives to kill all their baby boys.

Two midwives refuse to kill the babies. They let the boys live. This starts a revolution.

One specific baby who is saved from death is later adopted by the daughter of the Pharaoh. This baby, named Moses, grows up in Pharaoh's palace.

There is a great song by Louis Armstrong called "Go Down, Moses." I recommend it. My youngest son recommends it too. It's a family favorite. My son's name is Moses, actually.

Character development is key to a good story, and Moses' personal story weaves in and out of the community story in the Exodus. Consider his life moments the close-ups in the movie.

Moses grows up, and at some point he observes an Egyptian beating a Hebrew slave; he reacts violently and kills the Egyptian. He leaves Egypt as a fugitive and escapes to the desert, where he meets a community who become his family when he marries the chief's daughter. He becomes a shepherd in the desert.

The people of Israel cry out to God for deliverance. God hears them.

God appears to Moses in the desert through a burning bush. Moses hears God's call to him and responds.

God sends Moses to confront Pharaoh and deliver his

people from slavery. Pharaoh is not so keen. He is hard hearted and refuses to listen.

Moses listens to God and does what he says. It takes a long time and a lot of signs and wonders and talking and using a stick and praying and waiting—a long time and more than one person (Aaron and Miriam help Moses lead, for starters)—but the Israelites finally walk out of Egypt across the bottom of the Red Sea, which is miraculously parted for them to walk through and then released as the Egyptian army tries to bring them back. Boom.

The Israelites party hard and celebrate and build a monument and then start complaining because it dawns on them that they will most likely never survive the desert. Oh yeah—the desert again. Sense a theme?

The people of God spend forty years wandering around in the desert, learning how to represent God on earth and live a new way—not as slaves but as free people. It takes them a long time to get to the "Promised Land"—land they had been told in advance would be theirs. I'm hoping this book might help us all spend less time wandering around and more time living in freedom. God help us.

CHAPTER 1

Breathtaking Beauty

But the midwives had far too much
respect for God and didn't do
what the king of Egypt ordered;
they let the boy babies live.

EXODUS 1:17-18

WHEN MY YOUNGEST son was born, it was magical—not in the witchcraft kind of way but in the Walt Disney sort of tingles-down-your-spine, heaven-on-earth sort of way. Actually, if the truth be told (and why not tell it), I loved him before he was born. In the early ultrasound he looked a bit like a skeletal transformer, but even still, I loved him before we met.

Life and beauty are gifts. I'm not talking about the kind of beauty that is marketed and sold in bottles and formulas, but the kind that comes crying in a wrinkled and bloodied newborn body. Life in this most fragile form is a gift to the world—a sign of something greater, bigger, deeper. I talk to people all the time—strong and scary people, people with scars and leather jackets and a lot of tattoos—who say that the birth of a baby took all their pain away. All their resentments left them as they held a six-pound bundle of skin and bones. A baby who can't do anything for itself somehow allowed them to experience the gift of life. It took their breath away.

When they tell me their stories, I understand. It's my story too. Perhaps you know what I mean. It's not always a newborn baby; the gift comes in kindness and goodness expressed everywhere. It's there in beauty and hope revealed through small acts of life every single day.

Life has power. Beauty has strength. It's quite remarkable when you think of it, and it's important to remember.

I remember a man who was an alcoholic for years. He was unwanted and rejected, regularly escorted out of towns by the police. He told me about being in detox, trying to get better but shaking and feeling so very sick as the alcohol was leaving his body. Sick and alone, that part of his life was a blur. But he remembers something very clearly: A lovely nurse sat with him and held his head in her lap, caressing his hair as a mother might have done, had he ever had a mother who loved him. He said he just wept. He wept in the lap of love. As he recalled the story, he couldn't remember the last time someone had touched him with kindness.

That kindness impacted him. It was powerful, a force of love. He told me his story years later as my supervisor in The

Salvation Army, a wonderful man of God who fought every day for others, trying to spread goodness to a dark and lonely world. He was an incredible example of what one life—and the power of kindness—can do in the world.

This is what I love about the Exodus. The story God tells of the deliverance of his people from slavery in Egypt is a powerful one. It's not pretend or make-believe; it's dipped in the blood and guts of real life. The backdrop is almost entirely dark, actually, as though God understands better than anyone how difficult real life is. But the light and the power of beauty in it, the sheer force of love and goodness and truth, is mind-blowing. Kindness itself stands out against the dark backdrop with vivid, breathtaking intensity. In many ways the Exodus story is the story of life. It's the story of God's people being born. This story that begins in tragedy and slavery and bondage and fear is actually a story of birth and hope and kindness and beauty changing the world.

The Revolutionary Start

The Exodus didn't start when Moses stood before the Red Sea, waiting for it to part. It didn't start when Moses stood before Pharaoh, waiting for him to "let my people go." It didn't start when Moses stood before a burning bush or even when he stood over the body of an Egyptian slave driver he had just killed. Two women started the Exodus before Moses was even born.

Two women, in a world where women didn't really count

much. They weren't even Egyptian women—at least Egyptian women would have had some influence or power. But these were two simple Hebrew midwives. In the eyes of the world, their importance didn't really even register on a scale.

One day the raging and fearful king of Egypt, the Pharaoh whose name we don't know (the Bible's storyteller doesn't bother to mention it), asks these two Hebrew women to do something dark and horrible. He wants them to kill all the baby boys born to the Hebrews.

Now this is horrible in itself, but perhaps even more terrible to a people who have been taught the value of life. In the creation account of the Hebrews, people were valued not because of what they do, but because God created them. They are intrinsically valuable—just to be born is evidence of God declaring you *good*.

Pharaoh wouldn't have shared this worldview. For ancient Egyptians, people were functional. Women were property. Hebrew boys were a potential threat. I doubt Pharaoh's command was even very personal; evil rarely is. It was most likely a cold, rational decision: Hebrew baby boys were better off dead.

The Egyptian midwives of the time could possibly swallow Pharaoh's edict that these babies were unnecessary. And in fact our current culture can be convinced of reasons why children shouldn't be born. But ancient Hebrews could not. The Hebrew midwives knew something that the Egyptians didn't: They knew life was a gift. They knew babies don't come from storks, or the will of a man, or even the womb of a woman. Babies come from God. Life, the Hebrews have always taught us, is a gift.

So these two women did something incredibly powerful. They said no. And make no mistake: Every revolutionary act begins with a no. When the most powerless group of people in society stood up to the most powerful, something happened. Time suspended, things slowed down, the world flipped upside-down even if for a brief moment, and everything changed. Because of their belief in God and beauty and life, because they were willing to take a risk and do the impossible thing, to do the right thing no matter what it cost, light came into an impossibly dark situation.

We know the names of those two women; the biblical record makes sure of it. Shiphrah and Puah. Pharaoh's name is not so clear, but then, what's special about a king being a tyrant? But Hebrew midwives standing up to a tyrant king? Now that is something special indeed. They are named in eternity because they defied a tyrant king to honor the King of life. And they let the boys live.

In that season, a little baby was born to parents who saw that he was beautiful, special, valuable—something every parent would see if they had the eyes to see it. That baby grew up to be an unlikely hero, Moses, who would lead the people of God from slavery to freedom—an Exodus so big the world is still talking about it! He was a deliverer, first delivered by two women who understood the breathtaking power of beauty in life.

In the story of God's people getting free, the value of life is a central theme that I think would be irresponsible to miss. Shiphrah and Puah put their lives on the line for it. Moses' parents saw the value of their beautiful baby boy at his birth. Even Pharaoh's daughter, when she opened a basket floating on the Nile River and saw Moses' precious little face, understood that the power of life—the gift of it, the value of it—is a force. And now, when life is birthed, and the cry is heard, we are all reduced to tears—or maybe enlarged to tears, because the beauty of it unlocks something within us, and we weep in the lap of love. Touched by kindness. Breathtaking beauty.

This is how God sees us—as a gift to the world, as people with value and purpose and beauty. Not because of our gifts or our jobs or our bank accounts, but because of who we are. He made us with deep value.

Let that understanding guide you as you read this story. Because the Exodus is really everyone's story. Every single one of us struggles with the oppression of being devalued. Every single one of us faces choices like the one those midwives made on a completely normal day in Egypt many thousands of years ago. I'm praying that we would learn from their example and let the boys live on our watch, that life would have room to cry, grow, learn, expand in us and through us. May we be born again into the beauty of God's Kingdom of life. Right now. Our Exodus starts as we encounter the breathtaking beauty of life.

Your life.

All life.

Is a *gift*.

Finding Freedom

What are some of the things—the expressions of goodness and beauty and life—that take your breath away?

How are these expressions sometimes devalued by others?

What can you do to assert and celebrate their value?

CHAPTER 2

How Slavery Starts

And so Israel settled down in Egypt in
the region of Goshen. They acquired
property and flourished. They became
a large company of people.

GENESIS 47:27

SLAVERY IS A tricky business. It is estimated that there are more slaves in our world today than in all the years of the transatlantic slave trade put together—48 million is the popular estimate. Many of them don't even know they are slaves. I know several women who believe that the pimps and rapists who control their lives "love" them and help them.

This is one of the complicated things about slavery. Many people who are trapped in its grip don't even know it. One woman I spent a lot of time with over the years went on her own personal exodus from sexual slavery. It took years for it to sink in that she had lived a horrible and hard life. Up until her willingness to let Jesus guide her on a journey of remembering and feeling, she simply refused to admit the truth, because *she didn't want to be a slave.*

Nobody wants to be a slave. So even when we are, objectively, by definition, bound to and controlled by another, we are inclined to see our lives differently, to interpret reality in a way that avoids admitting the fundamental truth. Denial is a powerful thing. And the truth can be painful.

I saw a documentary on child exploitation in India. There are whole tribes who are enslaved to corporations making things like soccer balls and carpets and trinkets we buy. These tribes are enslaved for generations because somewhere along the way, someone needed a loan. Not an exorbitant amount of money, sometimes just fifty bucks, but the person who loaned it added huge interest until it ended up being a debt of hundreds of dollars—even after the initial borrower worked his entire life to pay it back. That debt becomes a "family loan," and the borrower's child is recruited to take the place of the father in the "workforce" to pay back the loan, still accruing interest. This is a circular, systemic trap: Children born into these households accept the reality that their whole lives will be spent in hard labor, paying off a loan that will never be paid. It's servitude. It's slavery. It's wrong. But how does the cycle stop? How does freedom come? How do women, children, and men get free?

Most of us find this kind of slavery impossible to believe, which is ironic, considering that *we are all slaves.* I know it's difficult to believe, but it's true: We are all enslaved to a

global system, a way of life, a tyrant Pharaoh of epic propor-
tions, and we don't even know it.

A few years ago I was studying the escape of the Israelites
from Egypt because I thought it would offer some signifi-
cant clues about freedom, and my own fight against human
trafficking was in need of some theological reflection. I presented what I was learning at a conference, where I ran into
an incredible man from Brazil, Claudio Oliver. He asked me
some very interesting questions about the Exodus, beginning
with this one: What kind of slaves were the Israelites?

That's easy, I thought. Everyone has seen *The Prince of
Egypt* and knows that the Israelites were *enslaved*. Images of
Israelites chained up and beaten by evil Egyptian slavers came
immediately to mind. The Israelites were slaves. Full stop.

Claudio began to gently ask some other questions, slowly
and graciously revealing my idealistic and shallow read of
the text.

What kind of slaves own their own homes?

What kind of slaves have their own livestock?

What kind of slaves have a representative who speaks to
the king?

What kind of slaves are threatening to the world's largest
superpower?

Whoa! Stop with the questions already. Talk about disrupt-
ing my mental image. So if they weren't chained up, if they
weren't locked down and depleted of their own resources, if
they weren't tied up and imprisoned, then how and when did
this happen and what kind of slavery is this?

Good question. Actually, this is the key question to Exodus and our own journey to freedom: *What kind of slaves were the Israelites?*

Thanks, Claudio. What I began to discover is that in the Exodus story, the person who calls the Israelites slaves is God. God reveals that the Israelites had become slaves to Egypt long before Egypt began to oppress them.

Were the Israelites oppressed in Egypt? Absolutely. Were they slaves? You better believe they were. But the story of slavery doesn't start with oppression. The story begins a lot earlier than that.

How It All Started

It helps to remember why Israel was even in Egypt. It's not like they were captured and forced to be in a heathen land. They were in fact saved by Egypt; more to the point, the Israelites had saved Egypt. The Israelites (Joseph in particular) had saved Egypt (from a famine) in order that Egypt might save Israel (from that same famine). Talk about a convoluted past.

Slavery is always a complicated story; slaves and slavers are often webbed together in shared life and history. If only slavery were as simple as bad guys and good guys, but these right-and-wrong categories of slavery hardly ever exist.

Israel, for example, was invited to stay in Egypt as honored guests of Pharaoh. Joseph, the son of Jacob (the patriarch of Israel), had saved Egypt from famine as its second in command under Pharaoh; under Joseph's leadership, Egypt grew into the superpower it had now become. You can read in the book of Genesis about how Joseph's brilliant tax system made Pharaoh an all-powerful and very wealthy king. Egypt had much to thank Israel for, and Pharaoh knew it.

So he invited Israel to settle in Goshen. Goshen was the "best land in Egypt" for shepherds (Genesis 45:17-18), which is what the Israelites were, a tribe of shepherds. But when we pick up the story after Joseph dies and a few generations pass, Israel has traded in their shepherd staffs for something much more lucrative: bricklaying.

Egypt was the biggest builder in the known world. We are still flying around the world to take a look at the past glories of Egypt's brick empire, the Pyramids. Wealth in Egypt was not built from shepherding; as a matter of fact, in Egyptian culture to be a shepherd was a low-level job. To work the land was considered slaveworthy. In the hierarchy of vocations, shepherding was next to garbage collecting. No one really wanted to do it. If you were interested in really making it in Egypt, bricklaying was for you.

We don't really know how and when this happened. Well, we have a hint from Egyptian records that an old guard of Egyptian power always disliked shepherds and considered them vulgar and illiterate. Joseph served a Pharaoh from the "new order" of politicians, referred to as "shepherd kings." After Joseph died, the old order of Pharaohs came back to power. Slowly, history suggests, the value-base of Egypt shifted. Shepherds were back on the low-level list.

Socially, I wonder how it played out. How did the slow change of values begin to affect the Israelites? Was it the kids of the Israelites who went to school with Egyptian children and learned the hierarchy of social order and acceptability? Did they become ashamed of their parents' occupation? Their humble origins? Maybe they didn't invite people over for fear of their friends mocking the smell of livestock left in their house after a long day's work?

And so, the children began to think of a different way to live. A better way. A more lucrative way. A way of earning not only a better income but also prestige and power and influence. And what better way than getting into the building industry during the world's biggest building craze?

And so it began. Slowly, Israel traded in their livelihood, their heritage, their identity.

For some bricks.

Finding Freedom

What values have you seen change around you?

How have they made it harder for you to be yourself?

Where are you tempted to trade in your identity to do something that will make you more prosperous or increase your social standing?

CHAPTER 3

Tiny Little Spider Bites

Moses said to God, "Who am I that
I should go to Pharaoh and bring
the Israelites out of Egypt?"

EXODUS 3:11, NIV

IN MY FIRST post as a leader of people trying to follow Jesus through a local church and mission, I was fairly successful. But that success left me feeling a bit empty. So people were coming to church—so what? How was that going to change the world? How was that going to impact a generation?

Now, don't get me wrong. I believe local communities of believers who are surrendered to living holy lives in the midst of the chaos and darkness of our world can change the world and impact a generation. Holiness runs straight through the deep pain of the world. The trouble wasn't with my local church; it was with me. I was living a sleepy, easy, comfortable life. And I knew that success somehow made me even more comfortable.

One night I had a dream—a terrible, wonderful dream that began to change everything for me. I was walking through a doorway into a new room. There was a spiderweb covering the doorway, but I didn't realize it; I just walked through without seeing it. In the corner of the doorway was a big, fat, hairy spider. I didn't see the spider, didn't realize that I had been bitten.

I entered the room and immediately began to feel incredibly tired. I looked around and saw a cot in the middle of the room. I went straight there and lay down. As soon as I gave into the fatigue, I became completely paralyzed. I couldn't move. I was still conscious—I could tell where I was and what was going on—but I couldn't lift a finger. I was completely alive, but asleep.

Before I knew it, tiny little spiders came from all over the room. From every corner they came pouring out. They began to devour me, one tiny little spider bite at a time.

As you can imagine, I awoke from the dream horrified. I was deeply impacted by this crazy dream. I immediately rebuked the dream and sent it back to hell where it belonged. But the dream kept coming.

After trying some other well-intended strategies (including sleeping with a Bible under my pillow), I called in some heavyweights to help me. I asked some prayer people I knew to have an intervention with me to get this dream out of my life. I knew it wasn't good to die in your own dream! So they gathered and we prayed. One of them suggested we should ask God for an interpretation of the dream. I thought it was pretty obvious already—the devil has a plan to kill me—but we asked the Lord anyway. To my complete surprise, God revealed something that would change the course of my life forever.

In my dream, I represented the people of God. The spider represented the "fat spirit" (comfort, the world). The cot is where we end up when we've been bitten by the world's spirit. Death is where comfort ends. But it's not death in a heroic way. It's a death by small, insignificant things. It's a slow and painful slide into the reality of slavery.

The slow, tepid pace of changing values is a major reason that slaves don't know they are slaves. Simply put, we spend time on things we value. Our values determine our time, energies, and efforts. We become enslaved to things we begin to worship.

How do you spend your time? I live in a culture where work is the prominent value. Money is the other one. Spending money, to be more specific. I know a lot of people who work in such a way that it smells of slavery. They hardly ever see their kids or their spouses, can't participate in community or church life, are absent when their friends need them—if they have any real friends.

Many of these people are working at least two jobs. Why do you work two jobs, I ask them? Money, money, money is always the answer. Why do you need more money? Once they get over the offense of me even asking the question,

they answer, "For my house, my truck, my car, my . . . stuff."
Stuff. Loads of it. Tons of it. Thousands and thousands of
dollars spent on big screens, sound systems, video games,
kitchen appliances, and on and on and on. It's all so enthralling. We get good-paying jobs and start living at a standard
that requires us to keep the job, or we up our standard so that
we have to work even more. Soon, instead of working to live,
we are living to work. We have become indebted to the very
system we thought would liberate us.

If you have eyes to see differently, you can see this cycle
of slavery evident in people's everyday lives. But they don't
know it.

I can't tell you how many people I've met who've lost it
all—kids, jobs, family, almost their own lives. When they
realized they were slaves, it hit them so hard that they gave
themselves over to hopelessness. Sometimes through the
empty bottom of bottles of alcohol, sometimes through
violence and drugs, sometimes just through depression and
suicide attempts. The whole thing, once you realize it, is
depressing.

I remember reading a little book by Tom Sine way back
when I first started ministry. In *The Mustard Seed Conspiracy*
he predicted a grim future where a whole generation of
people would become enslaved to money, work, and stuff.
It was the first time I ever heard anyone calling the situation
we were heading into (with all our motors running) slavery.
Unless we were deliberate about recognizing our condition
and choosing a different way, he argued, this would cause

a terrible reaction in world missions, the local church, and social change. Wow. He called it.

I remember him suggesting different ways to live. They were intriguing to me. It was the first time I considered shared housing and resources, even new designs for housing multiple generations under the same roof. It was incredible. What would it look like for me to aim for a different ending than the world prescribed? Instead of more money and more stuff (which would require more work), I started to aim for more time for ministry, more opportunity to serve and to give. Make less, give more.

It was like a Jerry Maguire moment, an "aha" of sorts. It was life-changing, and it made complete sense. Do you have any idea how many people would love to do exactly what Jesus asks them but are literally stuck with a mortgage and a car payment and a college fund? They can't go anywhere. Not just for a few years either, but for their whole lives. How could you change something that had you in the grip of its own system?

I had a student who came to live with our community for a year of discipleship training. Over the course of a few years he had racked up credit card debt in college; he was under such a huge load of debt that he could never imagine getting out of it. Is that not slavery?

Apparently this system is intentionally designed. Credit card companies target students because they see a future market. No kidding: a whole market of people becoming slaves without knowing it. The packaging of it looks like liberation.

Buy whatever you want now. Pay later. Welcome to the slippery slope of slavery.

After I read *The Mustard Seed Conspiracy*, I started thinking about living a different way. What would it look like for me to live differently from the dominant values of the world I was in? I started to realize that I was made to change the world, not to join it.

I wonder if Moses had thoughts like these? Joseph did. When Joseph went to Egypt in the very beginning, a literal slave in the prisons of that land, he knew *who he was*. He was special. He was chosen. He had a destiny that would bring salvation to people. This is a theme throughout his life story. And even when the conditions of his life were difficult on every level, he never forgot who he was. Even when Joseph was *prospering*, he remembered who he was, and it kept him alert to his spiritual purpose.

Maybe life is not just about the things we accumulate or what others think of us. Perhaps life is much more valuable than all of that. Perhaps we were created for a spiritual purpose. To be a blessing to the earth. To bring hope and freedom and truth and beauty to the world. What if life isn't a competition about which one of us is most important? What if every one of us is important? Freedom is found in this awakened understanding of our purpose. Slavery, by contrast, starts with a temptation to forget who we really are and why we are here.

The powerful movie *12 Years a Slave* tells how this process happens, in a painfully brilliant portrayal of the life of

Solomon Northup. When he is first captured, he keeps telling his captors his name. They tell him—well, they beat the lie into him—that is not who he is. They give him a new name: Platt. A fake name. A new identity. A slave identity. As the slow, oppressive force of slavery settles in, you can see the change in him. He comes into agreement with this new, fake identity. He starts to answer to his slave name. He starts to forget the memory of freedom. He stops using his gifts. He refuses to cry for his family. It's painful to watch. It's also painful to live.

All of us are born with value, regardless of the circumstances of our natural birth. We were born to change the world. We were born for freedom. Our task in life is to come into agreement with God about who we are. This understanding that our value comes from God and not from ourselves or the world around us is liberating at our core.

I've always wanted to be a missionary. I suspect this is because I intuitively think God loves missionaries more. (In the Christian hierarchy we never say this, but we sure mean it.) But once I read *The Mustard Seed Conspiracy*, I realized that I wanted to be a missionary in order to escape the oppressive culture I had become compliant with. The dominant spirit of money, greed, power, and control was so strong, so pervasive, that even though I saw what needed to happen and had a desire to live differently, I kept gravitating toward it. I didn't eat when I was hungry; I ate all the time. I ate what I felt like eating, not what my body needed. I watched copious amounts of television even though I didn't want to. I lived with my husband in a big house and didn't make room for those with no family or no home. I admired, with the rest of the world, the rich and the famous, and dreamed of becoming like them, thinking how great it must be to be them. I chose to believe that wealth meant success and success meant happiness and happiness meant bliss. And so I lived as though that's what I wanted. I was a slave to my own desire.

But this is the thing about slavery. Once you've swallowed this line of thought, slowly but surely the lie starts to kill you.

Willful Blindness

In her book *Willful Blindness*, Margaret Heffernan writes of an undercurrent present in so many moral decisions made by people in circumstances and situations from around the world: the brain's natural tendency to believe the truth we want to be true rather than truth based on evidence. From Nazi Germany's Holocaust to a husband's illicit affair, personal and corporate willful blindness leads to extreme moral breakdown and often disaster. Willful blindness allows horrible injustices and immoral decisions to go unchecked—think the US banking mortgage collapse or the Enron scandal. Heffernan powerfully suggests these breakdowns can be avoided when as few as one or two people stop conforming to the pattern of willful blindness.

Studying the traits of "whistle-blowers," Heffernan realizes that, far from troublemakers or pot stirrers, they are usually highly committed to the mission or cause at risk. They have an overriding desire for truth. They don't want to appear to be doing good; they really want to do good. And this leads them to decide for a deep moral integrity that can literally change the world.

I pray we will all be awakened to the tiny little spider bites that can lull us to sleep and lead us into slavery and death. The slide into slavery rarely comes in a glorious battle; more often it comes through small, incremental shifts in our thinking and living. The little compromises we make every day eat away at us. Nevertheless, they are based on and emanate from a big lie that we don't even notice we embrace: We surrender our identity at the door to the dominant image of the good life we're presented with. We accept the reality before us, even if it is in clear defiance of the reality God has invited us into. We settle into the values we've compromised and the lies we've embraced. We've lost before we even realize it.

Finding Freedom

How have your values changed over time?

What cultural values—money, success, beauty, stuff, or something else—have seemed to be a particular temptation for you?

What slippery slope do you need to guard against?

CHAPTER 4

What Pain Can Do

Many years later the king of Egypt died.
The Israelites groaned under their slavery
and cried out. Their cries for relief from
their hard labor ascended to God.

EXODUS 2:23

THE PAIN OF slavery is deep within all of us.

It was thought for years that leprosy somehow made people's limbs and extremities fall off. That was before Paul Brand, a missionary doctor who specialized in the treatment and causes of leprosy, discovered the loss of limbs and extremities was a *symptom* of the disease, not part of the disease itself.

An important characteristic of leprosy is that pain receptors do not work properly. People with leprosy can't feel pain. When you put it like that, it sounds like a great disease. But the reality is that without pain, bad things happen.

One of Dr. Brand's patients kept losing the ends of his

fingers. He didn't know why or how it was happening. So Dr. Brand decided to watch him for twenty-four hours. What he and his team discovered was horrifying. At night, when the man was sleeping, rats would come out of hiding and feast on the man's fingers. And because the man's leprosy had caused his pain receptors to not work properly, the man didn't feel a thing. He just kept sleeping as though nothing was happening. In the morning he had another finger partly gone. Wow.

Another patient, a young girl (not even two years old), was found by her parents in her crib one morning with blood everywhere. To their horror, they realized that she had bitten off her own fingers and was using the blood as a crayon to color her crib. They called in Dr. Brand; he was able to confirm that indeed she had leprosy. Her life was going to be incredibly difficult. She had to be restrained as a young toddler from inflicting harm on herself. She had to learn what pain was from a theoretical basis because she couldn't experience it for herself.

Dr. Brand became a huge fan of pain. He wrote a book with Philip Yancey called *The Gift of Pain*. It's a great read, very helpful because we've grown up learning to mask pain— to avoid it.

This is why the gospel call is so countercultural for us. Jesus actually invites us into a life of pain. He puts it like this: "Take up your cross daily, and follow me." The cross was not meant to be a funky necklace or a fashion accessory. It is a literal symbol for suffering and death, symbolic of the kind of message and ministry the gospel brings.

Jesus goes out of his way to encounter the pain of every-day people who live hard and horrible lives, who need hope and an answer. This is not easy to do, especially for people who have numbed themselves to pain.

Somewhere in the Exodus story, the Israelites started to become dissatisfied. It began to bother them that they had forgotten who they were. We don't get the details at the front end, but there are some hints in the story that allude to some important things.

For one thing, when Moses finally goes to Pharaoh and tells him to let the people go, Pharaoh asks by whose authority Moses is asking this. Moses says, "GOD, the God of Israel."

Pharaoh says, "And who is GOD? . . . I know nothing of this so-called 'GOD.'"

That's a powerful statement. There are over a million Israelites in the land of Goshen, and Pharaoh is threatened by the sheer force of the Israelites' numbers. But he has never even heard of Israel's God. How could that be? Perhaps when the Israelites forgot who they were, they also forgot who God was?

I'll never forget when I first heard and understood the story line from the Song of Songs in the Bible. There is a picture painted of a bride who has just gone to bed; she has washed her hair and her feet. She is tired and all tucked in. Her lover comes to the door and knocks, but she tells him to go away; she is tired and already in bed. Finally, the lover thrusts his hand through the door, and as she catches a glimpse of him, something changes. Struck by the reality of his presence at the door, she hops out of bed and answers it. Love has woken her from her comfy, sleepy place.

When she answers the door, the lover is gone, and the woman begins a long and painful pursuit to find him. On her way she is beaten and bruised, tired and hungry, until she finds him at last in a harvest field and they share a glorious embrace.

The symbols are extraordinary. What if we are the comfy, sleepy bride, and our lover is inviting us to go with him on an adventure of freedom and harvest? Would we get out of bed? God is like this lover: Even when we choose to sleep in comfort, God will not leave us alone. His love for us and the world he created means he's not satisfied to leave us in an oblivious sleepy state.

There is a haunting line from the movie *The King and I*. A woman has been chosen by the king to be one of his concubines (a great honor), but she is in love with a young man from her village. Despite their love for each other, they have to separate and are forced into lives of enslavement. The woman can't leave the king's palace. The man is so distraught that he joins a Buddhist monastery. Both are miserable.

So the woman makes a decision to disguise herself as a male monk in order to have one last time with her lover. At the risk of death, they have a deep, meaningful moment together before the police are sent to find her. While they are dragging her to her death, she says, "If love was a choice, why would anyone choose such excruciating pain?" It's a question that has always stuck with me.

Jesus modeled this kind of love. His story is a love story demonstrated by his willingness to sacrifice himself so we could be united with God. Jesus was compelled by love, and he invites us into that same story.

But we tell ourselves a different story. We sell ourselves on a "bless me now" gospel. Most of us don't completely sell out; we just tell ourselves that it's fine to put ourselves before the gospel in order to avoid pain. But the problem is that *pain is part of the gospel.* Jesus never undersold the cost of following him.

When I had the spider dream, I asked God how to wake up; I didn't want to die, not even in a dream and certainly not by thousands of spider bites. He showed me another picture—this time it was a real story—a memory of a time when I was driving home after working for the night. I was falling asleep at the wheel, so I turned up the radio as loud as it would go. Still I felt sleepy. I tried pinching myself next. Slapping myself after that. And finally I resorted to the worst thing of all: In the midst of a Canadian winter, I rolled down my window and stuck my head out. My eyebrows were frozen and I couldn't feel my nose—but I was awake! And that is exactly what I needed to be. This uncomfortable, even painful action saved me from death by sleep.

Discomfort can wake us up to God's love. And God's love compels us to self-sacrifice for the sake of bringing freedom to the world. This is the great and beautiful cry of God's people: not a "bless me now" kind of love but a love that is willing to die for freedom. This cry begins with an acknowledgment that all is not right with the world. It culminates as we cry out to God to save us from our own self and sense of indulgence and sleepy spirits.

Inviting pain into our lives is not natural, but it can be helpful. Pain is part of the way we know we are alive. I'm not suggesting that pain is inevitable or desirable. I am not a fan of pain. But for those of us in the Western world, much of our personal pain is the direct result of selfishness and greed. It's because of the deep brokenness of the world that pain even entered it. What I am suggesting is that God can use the pain we feel to wake us up. He can even use the pain of others to awaken us to the urgent need for action.

The pain of the Israelites' oppression in Egypt woke them up to how far they had journeyed away from God's intention for their lives. This is what pain can do in the hands of God. It can have a redemptive effect. It can wake us up.

Rosa Parks kicked off the civil rights movement by refusing to get out of her seat and move to the "colored" area at the back of a Montgomery bus. Standing up to oppression would be painful, but she embraced the pain of it. Her life would never be the same. Many years later a journalist asked her why she picked that day to refuse cooperation with the systemic oppression of a segregated bus system. She said simply, "I was tired." The journalist filled in the blanks by asking if she was exhausted after working so hard all day and simply didn't have the energy to move. She responded, "Not that kind of tired. . . . I was not tired physically, or no more tired than I usually was at the end of a working day. I was not old, although some people have an image of me as being old then. I was forty-two. No, the only tired I was, was tired of giving in."

Finding Freedom

Where are some areas of life that you're "tired of giving in"?

Where might God be trying to wake you up?

What do you need to do to move toward the pain in your journey toward freedom?

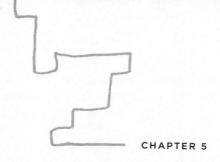

CHAPTER 5

Unlearning

Then he said, "I am the God of your
father: The God of Abraham, the
God of Isaac, the God of Jacob."
Moses hid his face, afraid to look at God.

EXODUS 3:6

MOSES GAINED THE world and then lost it. It's a fascinating journey if you think about it. Joseph was raised in a desert to lead in a palace, but Moses was raised in a palace to lead in a desert. We don't understand what it took to get Moses there exactly. We know some facts. He figured out he was an Israelite (or he knew this all along). He saw an Egyptian mistreating an Israelite and got angry, stepping in to defend him, striking the Egyptian, and killing him.

We can't figure out the exact details of the story. Was the Israelite at risk of death? Was Moses just mad, or was he actually scared about the outcome of the violence? Was Moses doing what he knew to do?

If ever there was someone justified in anger, it was Moses. Surely there would be a clause to let Moses off the hook for murder. We know that responding to violence with violence is inevitably destructive to everyone involved. Moses was no exception. Overnight Moses became a fugitive of the Egyptian justice system, and everything changed. This became part of the problem. Now Moses wasn't just sleeping with the enemy, he *was* the enemy. He had become the oppressor to the oppressor.

It wasn't so much that Moses was in Egypt that was the problem. It was the Egypt in Moses that was the issue. Moses left Egypt and began a process of learning how to live outside of Egypt. Not just the physical borders of the land, but the privilege and finery, the comfort and the ease of his lifestyle. This happened in the desert, as Moses began to lose his customs, his ego, his success, and his palace rights. This process would be repeated for all the Israelites—and for all of us who follow Jesus—because oppression isn't just something that happens to us from outside forces. Oppression happens inside of us too.

For Moses to encounter God, freedom, and the fearlessness to confront oppression, he had to get free *inside*. It would require an emptying before he could be filled, an "unlearning" of things he'd learned that were not helpful to his new life. He had to unlearn his privilege and let go of his ego.

If Egypt is anything like our world, it's success-driven. The better you perform, the better you are. Your value is based on your outcomes. This drive makes slaves of all of us.

To get to a place where you reject that reality usually requires a fair bit of desert and a whole lot of empty.

Janis Joplin once sang, "Freedom's just another word for nothing left to lose." I think she had that part right. There is some kind of freedom in getting to the end of yourself.

In his book *The Cost of Discipleship*, Dietrich Bonhoeffer famously wrote, "When Christ calls a man, he bids him come and die." He wrote this eight years before he followed Jesus to his own death at the gallows in Germany at the hands of the Nazis. He had opportunity to escape Germany; he had been invited to live in comfort, developing theology, writing, and preaching in New York—a pastor's life, an easy life, in America, safe—while Germany's future was still being determined. While his fellow ministers were languishing under the grim realities of Nazi power.

His American friends had sacrificed their reputations and their connections (and a fair bit of cash) to get him out of Germany. They had declared that God's will was for him to live, to use his gifts for the whole church. But Bonhoeffer had made a habit of reading the Sermon on the Mount, that bit of the Bible where Jesus speaks about the upside-down nature of the Kingdom of God. Bonhoeffer had made it a habit to hear the living Spirit of Jesus speak, and he was hearing Jesus say, "Come and die." And so against all the odds, and against all the wisdom of the world, Bonhoeffer went against the flow of the mass exodus out of Germany and entered into the midst of the flame. He tried to explain it to his American friends and benefactors, but he couldn't quite get them to understand.

Bonhoeffer was imprisoned with many others and lived a pastor's life after all. Only he pastored the people in the prison he was confined to—not just the other prisoners but also the guards. People say he was full of joy in those days as he joined Jesus in the cellblocks of the German Gestapo prison. Two days before the war was over, the guards led Bonhoeffer to the gallows. A fellow prisoner recalled his final words: "This is the end, but for me it is the beginning of life." Bonhoeffer died tragically and freely.

Bonhoeffer understood that the Kingdom of God comes through a different force than the world is used to. It's the same understanding that Jesus had in front of Pontius Pilate. Pilate declared to Jesus that he had power over his life. Jesus corrected him: "You haven't a shred of authority over me except what has been given you from heaven" (John 19:11).

This freedom in the face of worldly power is what Moses started to understand as he confronted Pharaoh. *Freedom* is just another word for *nothing left to lose.*

Catherine Booth, the cofounder of The Salvation Army, spent most of her preaching career warning the church about a powerless and false gospel growing in popularity. In her sermon "The Christs of the Nineteenth Century Compared with the Christ of God," she wrote,

> Men have made up their minds that they can possess
> and enjoy all they can get of this world in common

with their fellow-men, and yet get to heaven at last. They have made up their minds that it is all nonsense about following the Christ,—becoming a laughing stock to the world, which He made Himself every day He lived,—and setting themselves to live a holy life, which He said if they did not they were none of His; all this they have abandoned as an impossibility, and yet, not content without a religion, and finding it impossible to look into the future without a hope of some sort, they have manufactured a Christ to meet their views, and spun endless theories to match the state of their hearts. The worst of all, however, is that a great many of the teachers of Christianity have adopted these theories, and spend their whole lives in misrepresenting the Christ of the gospel.

I suppose we all expect people who follow Jesus to be different from the general public. I suppose we consider disciples and leaders of the way of Jesus to somehow be free from the oppression that the world suffers. When the news broke about priests molesting children, the world was rightly outraged. I remember reading that the percentage of pedophiles in the general population of America was roughly the same as the percentage of pedophile priests. For some reason, it didn't make me feel any better. What the world longs for is not more of the same, but something different: a people who embody something good. Freedom from the inside out.

But no matter what religious system we adhere to,

oppression has to be unlearned from deep inside of us. In the desert, away from Egypt, Moses was invited to a new way of leading. He had to be willing to lay down all that he had learned before in order to embark on God's invitation to do something that couldn't be done any human way.

I remember watching *Beyond the Gates of Splendor*, a documentary of the life of Jim Elliot. It's a remarkable story. He and his four missionary friends were killed as they tried to share the gospel with the Aucas in a remote area of Ecuador. Jim's wife, Elisabeth, eventually followed with her child in a canoe, to tell the Aucas that she forgave them. It turned out that the tribe was notoriously violent. Every family line had ended in tragic violence that was reciprocated and escalated with every new assault. The tribe was literally killing themselves off. God broke the cycle and ended up redeeming the whole tribe because one woman—a widow, with her child—decided to follow Jesus into the pain of her loss, giving him the potential of her own death and the future of her child.

At the end of the documentary there is a conversation between the man who killed one of the missionaries and the missionary's son. The man "adopted" the son as his own; the son called him uncle. The uncle was expressing his deep remorse and started weeping as he blurted out, "I'm so sorry I took your father's life."

The son stopped him and replied gently, "You didn't take his life. My father gave it." It's a powerful correction and an important one.

The world's way is power. It's force. But God's way is

through our weakness, our dependency, our obedience to his ways—even if it looks like certain death. Indeed, even if it *is* certain death. We know that God's Kingdom advances in ways we can never understand and that even the power of death cannot defeat God's Kingdom come. If we can grasp that, then we are truly free.

Moses had to learn the Kingdom way. We glimpse a "reckless" freedom in Moses as he keeps confronting the world's superpower and the most powerful man on the planet. Over and over again, Moses confronts Pharaoh, and every time he risks his own death. And every time he is in complete dependency on God. And God shows up.

Contrast this to when Moses tried the world's way. Perhaps he only knew of his God theoretically, not personally. After all, his whole life had been about control and power. He had been raised in a palace. He tried to take care of injustice in his own strength, and he became the oppressor. In the U2 song "Peace on Earth," Bono sings, "You become a monster so the monster will not break you." Violence begets violence, and even the best of us succumbs to our own attempts to justify ourselves and make ourselves look good at the expense of others. It's only God who can bring about his purposes in his own way for his own glory.

How many times have you discovered that you are actually standing in your own way? Old habits die hard. Old thinking seems entrenched. Long-held fears are holding tight, and opening up to new possibilities and new story lines seems impossible.

There is a prayer that many people in twelve-step recovery say in the hope of having a new experience. Here's one version of it:

God,
Please help me set aside
everything I think I know
about myself, my brokenness,
my spiritual path, and especially you;
so I may have an open mind
and a new experience of all these things.
Please let me see the truth.
Thy will be done.
Amen.

When we are interrupted from business as usual, with a confrontation of our ego—our lack of ability to actually change the world—the God of Abraham invites us to empty ourselves and learn a new way. We will find this new way at the end of pride. When we finally decide to unlearn the things of Egypt and embrace the way of Yahweh, like Moses we take off our sandals and bow before God, and we can begin to see our world shift toward freedom.

Moses finds freedom as he embraces the posture of a servant. His bare feet hit the dirt. He bows. He kneels before the God of his fathers and surrenders his achievements, failures, potential, hopes, dreams, and regrets. This is now much bigger than Moses. Let the unlearning begin.

Finding Freedom

What do you need to unlearn in order to move more into the Kingdom way?

What can you set aside to make the way more clear?

CHAPTER 6

There's a Pharaoh in All of Us

Yet Pharaoh was as stubborn
as ever—he wouldn't listen to
them, just as GOD had said.

EXODUS 7:13

WHEN WE READ the story of Exodus, why do we always assume that we have the most in common with the Israelites? This book is attempting to take the principles of freedom and apply them to our current lives, in order to make sure that liberation is *for* our real lives. But part of that journey is getting honest about who we are and what kind of oppression is threatening our own futures. What if we aren't the Israelites? What if we are the Egyptians? How would we interpret this story if we weren't the underdogs crying out to God, but we were the arrogant oppressors confronted with the God of the oppressed? We would do well to consider this possibility.

I just visited Tennessee. Before I hopped on a plane back to Los Angeles, I was able to stop by a historic plantation in Franklin. It was the site of a major battle in America's Civil War. It was long past the turning of the tide in the war—the Confederate forces knew their time was up—but they were going to die trying to win. Literally. Men and boys, husbands, fathers, and sons died in a virtual slaughter as they continued to charge the Union forces, outnumbered, outgunned, and ill-advised.

I was visiting the plantation as race riots in Charlotte, North Carolina, dominated the news. The Black Lives Matter movement was gaining momentum, and tensions were abounding in a racially divided country. I figured I should get a glimpse of the root of the problem. I had made the visit to the plantation to learn about slavery. I was trying to understand how people could have participated in the act of slavery as a matter of everyday life.

A hot and sticky day but a picturesque site waited for us as we stepped out of the minivan and onto rolling verdant hills with big green Osage trees offering shade in strategic places. I entered the welcome shop and asked for a brochure with a map to help me find my way around. That's when I realized that there was a strange sort of spirit about the place.

There was virtually no mention of slavery. The timeline on the brochure listed the dates when the homestead was built and the plantation started, and then the start of the war, then the battle, then the "end of the Civil War." There was no mention of slavery in the timeline. There was an example of the slave/servant quarters, which looked fine in a museum type of way. I kept re-reading the timeline and started looking around at the other guests. We were all white.

I made my way to the cemetery, where the soldiers who had "fallen" for the Confederacy were reburied in a dignified fashion, in a pristinely kept graveyard with marked graves, complete with flowers and iron gates and manicured lawns. This is all paid for and kept up by the United Daughters of the Confederacy. The brochure indicated that several of the scattered, unmarked, and untended graves might be where some of the "help" had been buried.

I looked everywhere for the plaque that acknowledged the pain and suffering of captured and sold human beings from another part of the world. I tried to find an apology or a lesson learned from the painful history of the slavery system of the Southern states. I searched to find a timeline of when the slaves were brought here, how they came, and when and how they left. But there was none. It wasn't mentioned. No apology. No acknowledgment. Slavery was simply treated like the old homestead: a historical, neutral fact. Nothing wrong here. The real tragedy of the Franklin plantation, according to the brochure, was the fallen soldiers, the humans who had been killed defending the right of the South to keep other people enslaved.

I know it sounds like I'm biased. And perhaps I am. I'm a student of slavery and freedom. But all the elements of this visit screamed denial to me. The unacknowledged pain and suffering, the unkempt, unmarked graves of the "other lives" lost in the South's history of slavery and suffering. It's as if the people who run that historical site are unaware of their own oppressive history. It's as if, even after the sacrifice of their young men, their hearts remain hard to their own complicity, their own sin.

I guess this visit hit me hard because I was remembering my visit to Robben Island off the coast of Cape Town, South Africa, where Nelson Mandela was kept for most of his twenty-seven years as a political prisoner by the apartheid government. Upon his election as the new president of South Africa, he opened Robben Island as a "university" where anyone could come and learn the painful lessons of oppression in order that we might not let it entangle us again. See, Nelson Mandela understood that unless the truth was told and acknowledged, it would simply be repeated. His heart was soft, bent to the higher purposes God had for him and his country. He instigated the Truth and Reconciliation Commission for victims and agents of apartheid alike to tell the truth and embrace a united future together. It was hard. It was horrible. It was, well, the most incredible thing the world had witnessed.

A friend of mine, a white South African woman, is writing a book about her shame and the process of healing from being part of a white supremacy system that caused so much suffering. She talks about wishing her skin were a different color. Her healing came through the shameful and painful acknowledgment of her part and privilege in a system that put her first at the expense of other people who didn't share her pigment. For the hard-hearted, here is either a bending or a breaking.

My visit to the Franklin Plantation was even more poignant, however, because of a friend who came with me. My friend Taanis is a strong, beautiful First Nations (North American Indian) woman. While I was frantically poring over the map to try to find a line or picture or acknowledgment about slavery, Taanis sat in the shade of a big Osage tree and prayed. She told me later that she felt the prayers of other people who had sat under that same tree and found the words to offer up a prayer for help, for meaning, for deliverance. She said she had only found one word to pray herself: *Why?* That one word—the sheer weight of the prayer—left us silent for a while on the drive to the airport. Why, indeed. Why do we oppress each other? Why do we harden our hearts? Why do we allow ourselves to be broken instead of being bent toward God? Why won't we acknowledge our pain, sin, guilt, and shame so we can be free?

As much as I want to identify with the Israelites, it would be its own subtle form of denial to suggest that's the only way the Exodus story applies. The truth of it is much different.

Right now, our entire Western economy thrives still at the expense of the poorest of the poor. Women and children in India and Bangladesh, far removed from our view, toil in cotton fields, often unpaid as slaves, so I can buy a T-shirt for five dollars. That purchase saves me enough cash to buy a cheap coffee picked by farmers in Ethiopia and Papua New Guinea who were ripped off by someone whose name and company I don't know and don't care to know, because what I care about more than people who can't afford to feed their family is that I can have a chocolate donut with my coffee. And don't even get me started about the cocoa that made that donut, picked by children enslaved on cocoa plantations on the Ivory Coast of Africa. Most of those child slaves have been trafficked from Mali because they are extremely poor and vulnerable to the worst forms of oppression. But who really cares, because nothing goes better together than chocolate and coffee.

So slavery is still stitched into my clothes and cooked into my food and drink, and I forgot to mention it on the brochure of my hard-hearted life. Meanwhile, America is building more prisons, effectively enslaving people of color, as argued with dazzling candor by legal scholar Michelle Alexander in her book *The New Jim Crow*: "We have not ended racial caste in America; we have merely redesigned it." A decades-long "war on drugs" is decimating communities of color, and the US criminal justice system relegates millions of people of color to a permanent second-class status—functioning as a contemporary system of racial control even as it formally adheres to the principle of colorblindness. Yet when I suggest that black lives matter, I'm called naive, even violent.

Could this story in our time have been different? I guess we'll see as we respond to the same God who hears the cries of the oppressed. There is a Pharaoh in all of us.

You can't hide from truth. You can't just pretend it didn't

happen or isn't important or has nothing to do with you. Well, you can for a while, if you want to be Pharaoh. Take a moment to be in the head and heart of the most powerful person on the planet. A person who has accumulated wealth and power by exploiting people. One day a shepherd marches in and, in a prophetic announcement, says God is on the side of the oppressed; it's time to let them go.

Are you shocked? Amused? Bewildered? Do you respond with an immediate acknowledgment of guilt and shame? Do you apologize?

No. You dig in. You prepare to fight for your right to your kingdom that you built. You protect your wealth and your spoils. You come up with righteous indignation at the sheer thankless audacity of a slave to confront your leadership. You slip into denial and defense, which is another way of saying you harden your heart, because the truth will be painful and shameful and hard. And it might cost you something. So you forget about it and tell yourself that *those people* should be glad they got to be part of your economic system and they don't even have it that bad and they have never even thanked you for all you've done for them.

What if you are Pharaoh? What if we are Egypt? How would we read the Exodus story differently? How would it feel to hear the words of God to Moses and Moses to us? What would it feel like to hang on to our pride at the expense of our own sons?

Maybe we make it about the fight, about the blood of our sons. Maybe we make it about the hardships we experience when the slaves finally go free, when we are left picking up the pieces, trying to stay king. Refusing to acknowledge where we are Pharaoh, where we are Egypt, is its own enslavement—enslavement to a lie. All the great reformers of history saw liberation extending beyond the oppressed to result in redemption of the oppressor, and the reconciliation of both.

We do all kinds of damage to ourselves and the people around us when we live in denial of our involvement in oppression. Denial—simply lying to ourselves—is a strange but true phenomenon that all of us deal with; we all have a bent toward denial. "I don't spend much money." "I'll work out later." "I won't get caught." "This won't hurt me." You may recognize the first instance of denial way back in a little story about the creation of humanity, when human beings denied what God said and did what they wanted anyway. Denial lies deep within our human condition.

And denial often works for us. Those of you who have ever done difficult physical training for a race know that denial is a fantastic tool for telling your body to keep going when it is clearly distressed. It can also override shame and fear, as a lesser evil that many of us can live with.

The problem with denial is when it feeds a negative behavior or a negative consequence. It becomes an even bigger problem when it's a group denial. If you are surrounded by a group of people who think, experience, and share the same things in common, it's quite possible that you are in denial together.

Part of my ministry over the last decade has been visiting brothels in Canada as a chaplain. It has taught me a lot about denial and its role in oppression. The rhetoric in legalized massage parlors in Canada is all about empowerment. The women in the parlors have been told and taught that they are completely empowered. They are exercising their God-given right to sell their bodies and make heaps of cash. Many of them have bought into this lie. When I first visit a place, this is the primary response from the women: "We love our work."

I remember one conversation very clearly—it was with a woman who operated (and worked in) a brothel in Edmonton, Alberta. It was a fairly run-down establishment, known for its "loose standards." The woman met me and my team at the door and promptly told us we weren't welcome. I didn't normally do this route, so her response wasn't un-expected. But I suggested that I needed her help: I was new to the city and didn't understand how the industry worked or how to help women. Would she help me? She responded, and we became good friends.

I was visiting the day this woman's daughter turned nine-teen. She was lamenting the fact that her daughter hadn't decided what to do with her future. I wondered out loud why she wouldn't just take over the "family business," now that she was of legal age. That comment didn't go well. My friend freaked out—I've never heard some of the words she used to describe what she would do to anyone who dared to offer her daughter a job in the industry. I guess it's not that empowering to work in a brothel after all.

What I encountered in those early visits was *denial*, a powerful tool we use to keep our oppression from getting us down. But don't even get me started on the denial the men who use the facility engage in. When guys are caught buying sex from a prostituted woman, they often suggest a lot of reasons why it isn't a big deal. You can read a great book by Victor Malarek called *The Johns: Sex for Sale and the Men Who Buy It* for a full picture, but suffice it to say that excuses range from "I was doing my part to help her make a living" to "She loved it" or "I'm not doing anything wrong," and on and on. A friend of mine runs a thing called "John School," a diversion program for first-time offenders who want to avoid the official process of the court (and a criminal record). John School takes a whole Saturday to complete and includes a fine. The most important part of the day is when a woman comes in and tells her story of exploitation. It changes everything. All of the lies, the denials, the false pretense of innocence fade away, and the johns are confronted with the cost to real human beings.

The woman tells a familiar story for those of us who are aware of the oppression of prostitution. She was abused as a child. She was a runaway and couldn't pay the bills. She was forced to sell her body to men to survive. She hated it. It hurt her—physically, mentally, and spiritually. She hated *them*. She was repulsed by all of them. She hated her life and wanted to die. My friend says the men change the moment they hear the truth.

That program has an unprecedented rate of recidivism:

Ninety percent of the guys who go to that one-day school never pay for sex again. I think it's because they've finally heard the cry.

There is no denying the truth when you hear the cry. Pharaoh refuses to hear the cry; God instinctively does. When he meets Moses, God refers to himself as the God who hears the cry (see Exodus 3:7). And it's not the first time the Scriptures use that term (see, for example, Genesis 21:17). God is the opposite of aloof, uncaring, unfeeling, and disconnected. He is moved to action because he hears his people. He is the God who hears the cry. Do you?

When we are in the thick of denial, we cannot get help. This is the most frustrating aspect of slavery and the sure nail in the coffin of its grip on our lives. Will we relent in our denial and accept the invitation God gives us to change our minds and behavior? Will we humble ourselves to hear the cry of the oppressed at the end of our lifestyles? Are we willing to make the costly changes to allow oppression to loosen its grip on those affected by us? Will we break or will we bend? There is a Pharaoh in all of us.

Finding Freedom

Where do you find glimpses of the Pharaoh in you?

Who do you know who can help you leave behind denial and bend toward God's Kingdom way?

CHAPTER 7

It Gets Worse before It Gets Better

Pharaoh . . . sent down orders to the slave-drivers
and their underlings: "Don't provide straw for the
people for making bricks as you have been doing.
Make them get their own straw. And make them
produce the same number of bricks—no reduction
in their daily quotas! They're getting lazy. They're
going around saying, 'Give us time off so we can
worship our God.' Crack down on them. That'll
cure them of their whining, their god-fantasies."

EXODUS 5:6-9

ONE OF THE weirdest moments in the Israelites' long walk to
freedom is when they start complaining about the food God
provided in the desert (Exodus 16). It's weird on so many
levels. I've heard a few sermons on this particular passage,
and they mostly say the same thing: The Israelites were so
ungrateful that they forgot how bad their slavery was. They
tricked themselves into thinking slavery was better than a
bland meal of manna.

The thing is, as we've come to discover, the Israelites might well have had it pretty good in Egypt for a long time. Until the oppression threatened to overcome them, they were working in the known world's largest growing market, living in their own homes, and raising their own livestock. They probably liked what they ate and now missed the variety of the fine foods of Egypt they used to have.

I've got a hunch their complaint wasn't only about the quality of food available in the desert. It might have also related to the *quantity*.

God told the Israelites to collect what they needed for each day. Anything more than that would go rotten. And it did. People hoarded the manna, and it rotted on the spot.

This unique training experience was teaching the people of God not just about God's provision but about the way he provides. He provides *what we need*. When we take more than we need, something always rots.

Egypt had taught the Israelites the exact opposite of this Kingdom value. Egypt had taught the Israelites to provide for themselves, to be tightfisted, to take. *Closed-handed living* is what I call it. It's how tyrants thrive.

Slavery always teaches people to take. We are taught a stingy survivor spirit, to take everything we can, anytime we can, by all means necessary. Mother Teresa once told a reporter not to blame poverty on God; terrible poverty exists, she said, simply because God's children refuse to share. And she's right.

What if everything we didn't need rotted on the spot? Can you imagine the maggots?

The Egyptians actually gave the Israelites all their treasures when they left Egypt. We don't hear much about Egypt after the Israelites' escape, but I think it's safe to say that Egypt learned the lesson of openhandedness the hard way.

Learning to live a different way is always harder than you think. And it always gets worse before it gets better. Freedom is a long walk. Ask Nelson Mandela. He was imprisoned as a political prisoner for twenty-seven years. And the cost wasn't just on his body. It was an attack on his entire life. His wife, his children, his future, his spirit, his hope—everything he went through was slavery.

But in his life story he talks about the long walk *to freedom.* The process began in prison: The ability to forgive, the eyes to see the good purposes in every human being, regardless of their color or their racial background, took root in him there. He began to dream of a completely different world, a world based on equality instead of color.

When you visit Robben Island, you are greeted by a tour guide who was a former prisoner there. This person takes you on a personal tour, with his own memories of his time there, to his old cell block and his old work camp placements. It's an amazing thing. At one point we all sat down in our tour guide's old cell; he told us we could ask him any question we wanted. People asked him some good ones, and then someone asked him, "What was the hardest thing about this prison?"

Our guide's answer shocked me. "Leaving this prison,"

he said, "was the hardest thing about it." We were dumb-founded. We had just seen what he had lived through at that prison. It was horrible. We couldn't understand.

He began to explain that he had come to the prison angry and frustrated and fearful. But he met some prisoners who taught him a new way to live. Now he could forgive and ask help and dream of another world. When he left the prison, he said, was when the real work began. He had to actually live a life of forgiveness and get to work building a new world. That was the really hard part.

He's right. One of the signs of freedom is that it gets worse before it gets better.

You can ask a drug addict going through detox. His life doesn't get better, and he will not be free, until he has gone through the pain of withdrawal and a rebuilding of normal. This will include physical and emotional pain—memories of hurt and repentance for the hurt he inflicted on others. It will include an acknowledgment of guilt and some restitution for wrongdoing. It will be a long walk, dealing not just with the effects of drug use on his body but the things that drove him to drug use in the first place. If we are honest, all of us need to deal with our sin the same way an addict deals with detox. The things that bring us freedom are often painful to experience.

In my own tradition of The Salvation Army, we have these incredible, miraculous stories of transformation. A few years ago I stumbled on William Booth's seven steps to salvation, which the early Salvation Army folks used to lead people to repentance and faith and relationship with Jesus. It's remarkable: Five out of the seven steps deal with sin. I'm not sure who you have led to Jesus and how you led them, but I rarely deal with sin with that kind of intensity. Sin often comes later, in what we would now call "deliverance."

I think Booth understood, though, that deliverance and salvation are deeply connected. This makes sense in a slavery perspective. If we are called from slavery to freedom, then a massive transaction has to take place: We have to be freed from both external and internal chains of slavery. We have to unwrap ourselves from our slavers. Salvation is an immersion experience. It is a whole-life posture. A giving over of our everyday selves.

There is a line of a famous song that says to God, "For thee all the pleasures of sin I resign." In recent years there was a bit of a commotion that "the pleasures of sin" is the wrong phrase. People suggested that sin couldn't be considered pleasurable. So there was a fight to change it to "the follies of sin." But I've got to say that there are things about sin that are very attractive (at least at first). And many sinful practices bring fleeting pleasure. Of course it doesn't last and leads to enslaved postures, but I like the idea of the original song for many reasons. Recognizing slavery as inherently evil is a beginning; but to relent from the practice of slavery and give up its benefits to us is equally important. The two must go together. Salvation and deliverance are the same process; they lead together to freedom from the inside out.

The BBC recently did a documentary on the largest government payout in history. It was connected to the parliamentary law change to abolish slavery that William Wilberforce and his friends had spent their entire lives fighting for. In the book *Amazing Grace*, one biographer of Wilberforce suggested the most powerful thing he did was change people's minds about slavery. Before him, people believed that slavery was morally excusable; after Wilberforce, slavery became illegal and immoral around the globe.

But in order to end legal slavery, the government had to get the elite and powerful families in Britain to agree to the new law. They had to buy them out. "The British government paid out £20m," it was reported by Sanchez Manning in the *Independent*, "to compensate some 3,000 families that owned slaves for the loss of their 'property' when slave-ownership was abolished in Britain's colonies in 1833. This figure represented a staggering 40 per cent of the Treasury's annual spending budget and, in today's terms, calculated as wage values, equates to around £16.5bn."

The government paid these slaveholders out because they wanted to free the slaves and change the way the world worked, and they knew those people would never support the bill if they were to lose their economic stability. My British friends are outraged about this truth. They truly believed that it was simply a tipping point of moral outrage that turned the tide in the fight against slavery in Britain. But it turns out that freedom takes a lot of work and a long time—and it comes at a heavy price.

Is billions of dollars the equivalent of a civil war? That's how America toppled its slave trade—a high cost indeed. Freedom is never without cost. It takes a long time and requires much sacrifice and hard work. What we always long for is an easy and quick version of freedom. It's what I like to call the Disney curse: We equate life transformation and changes of heart and outcomes in the world to a magical fairy godmother who shows up at just the right time with the right amount of fairy dust. In movies, dramatic change happens quickly, because movies have a time limit. But in real life, things don't work like that. The reality of freedom is that it is costly. It takes a lot of time, work, and effort to walk a new way.

Surely we all know the cost of challenging and changing the way we live. When in your life have you found yourself pursuing freedom? What has been the cost for you? Was the pain worth it? From eating habits to anxiety management, freedom—whenever it comes—costs us.

If we could shake our Disney curse and stop thinking that freedom just magically happens with some fairy dust and a simple prayer, we would be able to walk the long walk ourselves and accompany some others on the journey too. Encouraging them with a great cloud of witnesses echoing our words with their lives, that while it gets worse before it gets better, to be sure, it does get better. And when all is said and done, the journey to freedom is completely worth it.

Finding Freedom

How susceptible are you to the Disney curse?

What scares you about the prospect of greater freedom in your life?

What would help you have courage to face the hard parts of journeying toward freedom?

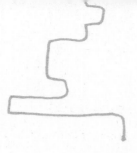

CHAPTER 8

The Wild Gospel and Living in Deserts

Moses agreed to settle down there with the man, who then gave his daughter Zipporah (Bird) to him for his wife. She had a son, and Moses named him Gershom (Sojourner), saying, "I'm a sojourner in a foreign country."

EXODUS 2:21-22

WE HAVE AN insatiable appetite for the positive. I've seen more than one offer to be "saved" presented as a means to be happy and wealthy. It's funny that the Bible doesn't seem to follow suit. Almost every major figure in Scripture has a tragic story—and often a tragic ending. Their lives, as a direct result of choosing to follow God, led them to difficult circumstances. Granted, they did live adventurous and full lives, but they weren't exactly poster people for happiness.

I'm writing this chapter during Lent, the forty days given to preparing our lives and hearts for the events of Easter in the Christian tradition. But of course we borrowed this idea of preparation from the Jews and their preparation for Passover.

The Exodus story gives us the first ever Passover, remembered as a festival every year since the eve of the Israelites' deliverance from Egypt. Faithful Jews prepared for Passover by getting rid of everything in their house that had yeast in it. Yeast came to represent sin and slavery and oppression; the idea was to live completely free of it in anticipation of their deliverance.

To kick off Lent, Christians often use the Scripture where Jesus is tempted in the desert (or wilderness). Most likely this is because Jesus spent forty days and nights there. But maybe there are other reasons; for instance, maybe this story about Jesus reminds us of the Exodus story, which starts in a desert with a man named Moses, who found hope there. Maybe we read this Jesus story because his forty days in the desert mirrors the time (forty years) the Israelites spent in the desert after being delivered from oppression in Egypt. The desert represented a time of testing for Jesus, which of course the Israelites experienced as they crossed the desert toward the Promised Land—a short trip that turned into forty long and mostly stupid years.

Jesus embraced his desert experience as a means of living a truly surrendered life. But the Israelites resisted it—they hated the desert. Israel resisted the desert experience so much that they spent most of their lives walking around in circles, complaining and setting up towns that they named things like "Bitter" (Exodus 15:22-24). Someone once said it took about a year to get Israel out of Egypt but forty years to get Egypt out of Israel. They wasted a whole generation resisting the process of "emptying."

In Genesis 1 the Spirit hovers over a sea of nothingness, out of which God creates. The process of emptying is how we get to our own place of nothingness out of which the Spirit can create something new in us. This is a difficult concept to understand and embrace, but it's woven through Scripture as a part of our faith journey. Embracing the desert places is a sure way to move deeper into the things of God's Kingdom come.

The Spirit led Jesus to the desert; the Spirit found Moses in the desert; the Spirit led the Israelites into the desert. For Jesus, this leading took place right after he was baptized—which is, to be honest, a bit weird. Jesus had just embraced his divine calling to be the Messiah. He had immersed himself (literally, by his baptism in the Jordan River) in the human condition in order to fight through the muck and the mire of our paralyzing internal oppression (often referred to as "sin") and to model a life lived fully. It was a bit of a rock-star moment: The heavens parted, a dove settled on him, and a voice from heaven affirmed his acceptance by the Father. That's got to be a good day! Maybe the best day. Ever.

Can you think of a day like that? When everything goes right? Seriously, a top-of-the-mountain moment, when you know deep inside yourself that you've heard the Father's blessing—even God is proud of you! This might be what the Israelites experienced after the Red Sea parted and the Egyptian army fell into complete defeat.

After a moment like Jesus' top-of-the-mountain moment of baptism, if you were interested in changing the world, you'd most likely stage a press conference—or head straight to Jerusalem to announce to the world powers that be there is a new King in town. Something dramatic and public— at least you'd head home and tell your mom, "I told you so!" But the Scriptures tell a different story, a strange story: *Immediately* after Jesus was baptized, the Spirit led him into the wilderness (Matthew 4:1). The wilderness. Really.

Like Jesus, Moses and the Israelites end up in the desert almost immediately after celebrating their top-of-the-mountain moment: Egypt's army, drowned in the Red Sea. But unlike Jesus' trip to the desert, as soon as the Israelites finished their song and dance, the complaining began. Murmuring gradually grew into a full-blown chorus of complaints: God had rescued them from slavery in order to kill them in the desert.

Now, I want to make fun of the Israelites, to at least poke fun at their lack of faith and thankfulness. But I have to be honest. See, I'm not sure about you, but I have a tendency to believe that everything that happens to me that is hard and horrible is from hell. The trouble is, I tend to designate as "hard" and "horrible" anything that is difficult and testing.

You can almost hear the Israelites complaining with every long process, or waiting moment, or thirsty time, or having to share or treat one another with equality and fairness. Or having to walk when they feel like stopping. You get the idea. The desert was forming the Israelites into God's likeness. It was a boot camp of spiritual preparedness to represent God to the world. This is what God's Kingdom way looks like: It looks like everyone having what they need, not taking what they want. It looks like people making room for others. It looks like humility. It looks like obedience to God. It looks like perseverance and faith through hard times. All of these things bring deep spiritual authenticity and credibility. None of it—let's face it—is sexy.

If we are honest, the things that we would rather do to represent God to the world are connected to what the devil tempts Jesus to do in the desert.

1. Turn stones into bread (Matthew 4:3). We are tempted to use our gifts for ourselves rather than for others.

2. Throw yourself from the highest point of the Temple (Matthew 4:5-6). We are tempted to be spectacular—to always aim for a big production, a public display. Power.

3. Become King of the World now (Matthew 4:8). We are tempted to skip the pain and compromise the process. Any means necessary for the desired outcome.

What is striking about the temptations themselves is how closely they align with Jesus' destiny. The devil never once questions whether Jesus is truly the Messiah, whether he is coming to establish his Kingdom, whether he is going to change the world. He only tempts Jesus in the *way* to do those things.

Jesus resists the tempter because he knows that the way he brings the Kingdom is as important as the arrival of the Kingdom itself. As Melissa Etheridge sang—and I recently found out is actually a quotation from an old, saintly woman, Catherine of Siena—"All the way to heaven is heaven." Jesus resisted the big and glorious things of the world—power and money and fame—while embracing small towns, small people, small followers. He celebrated the way of the Kingdom of God—not the applause of humanity but the loving voice of our Father, proud as punch of who we are.

The Israelites, by contrast, resisted this with almost a comical ferocity. They kept looking for big, glorious moments; they wanted shiny, and they wanted it *now*. They wanted more and bigger and status and . . . well, I could go on. They were stumbling and bumbling through the basic training of Kingdom living. So am I, if I'm honest.

We can spend a whole lifetime wandering around in a wilderness, pathetically unhappy in our faith, questioning God and making up little places to settle. We can miss the incredibly deeper experience of emptying. The devil wants to get us to follow Jesus, but in a worldly way. Leave Egypt, yes, but bring all of Egypt's values and systems with you. Be a Christian, yes, but live like everyone else. The devil tries to keep us full of ourselves. And this is problematic, because it's when we empty ourselves that God begins something new in us.

When Jesus came to the earth, Philippians 2 tells us, he emptied himself of, well, himself. And in so doing he embraced the calling to save the world. This emptying seems to be the only way we can avoid allowing ego, power, and success to dictate our lives and actions. In the desert, as we embrace the emptying process, we give God time and space to show us the things in us that are in the way. It's a surrendering. In a way, it's losing our life. And most of us are deeply disoriented by this process. We feel like to become better people we should be getting more: learning new strategies or developing new skills. The process God invites us into is a losing before a gaining. What others think of us can no longer define our decisions; that's the way of Egypt.

When John the Baptist saw that Jesus, the Messiah, was coming, he told his followers, "He must increase, but I must decrease" (John 3:30, KJV). Less of us is the recipe for more of God in our lives and in the world. But are we willing? How long will we resist the Holy Spirit hovering over our lives and creating a new thing in a new way? I imagine that process does not need to take forty years. How long will it take you?

Finding Freedom

Which of the devil's temptations in the desert is most tempting to you?

What can help you to embrace an emptying process so that God can do something new in and through you?

Can you think of some ways you resist the emptying process of the desert in your own life?

Who do you need to forgive in order to be free?

The End of Ourselves

For who were the people who turned a deaf
ear? Weren't they the very ones Moses led out
of Egypt? And who was God provoked with for
forty years? Wasn't it those who turned a deaf
ear and ended up corpses in the wilderness?
And when he swore that they'd never get where
they were going, wasn't he talking to the ones
who turned a deaf ear? They never got there
because they never listened, never believed.

HEBREWS 3:15-19

PEOPLE IN RECOVERY circles use some very helpful phrases
to describe the kind of behavior that keeps us from experiencing freedom—or for settling for external freedom while
still experiencing slavery on the inside. We get locked into
patterns of increased oppression because of "stinking thinking." We find ourselves, like Moses and Pharaoh at different
points in their lives, "on our knees," at the perfect spot: "the
end of ourselves." The end of ourselves—our running, our

lies, our excuses, our cycles of enslavement—is where the real freedom begins, from the inside out. We may get there, as a friend of mine always puts it, by way of "repentance now, or judgment later." But however we get there, it's a good place to be. Recently I heard a guy who was addicted to pornography and sex say it like this: "I got caught, and this was a great grace."

Finding the end of ourselves can take a lifetime. I guess it depends on your capacity for pain. But in case this sounds a bit too good to be true, let's consider together three things that stop freedom from coming.

The Geographical Cure

The geographical cure is famous as a means of escape. And escape is what people think they need to be free. Most of us, apart from folks who are trapped in external conditions of slavery, are not "kept" in our enslavements. They control us only insofar as we allow them to control us. Still, we think our external circumstances are the primary cause of our internal enslavements. The lie of the geographical cure is that if you only move to a different place, you will find a different, better reality. People do this *all the time*, in my experience. They keep moving to different places, thinking that will change their internal reality. If you are caught in old patterns, you should simply move to a new town, country, job, school, church; then everything will be different, right? Wrong.

The geographical cure never addresses the core problem: You can't run away from yourself.

G. K. Chesterton once wrote a response in a newspaper to a writer who asked, "What's wrong with the world?" His answer was, "I am." The trouble with the world is you. Until you stop running away from yourself, you can't get free. We see this with Moses, on the run from his past, his circumstances, his failures; we see him confronted by God in the desert many years later. Finally, Moses has to come to reconcile himself to himself. He cannot run away from his own life. He has to own it. And then, after the confrontation with God, Moses starts running to something instead of running away from things. He starts to head out with a purpose, with deep intention.

Are you running to something? Or are you running away? If you are tempted to believe that geography is your deepest problem, you are believing a lie. Our journey isn't defined by our geography. It's defined by us.

The Relationship Remedy

I can't tell you how much the relationship remedy gets in the way of real freedom. The lie goes like this: If it's not where you live, it must be who you live with. If you only had a different spouse, or different friends, or a different church, or fill in the different blank *ad nauseam*. This cycle of thinking will never end.

This particular lie puts the emphasis on the external

relationships you are in. It places the blame on other people. Believing that it's the people around you making you miserable allows you to let yourself off the hook yet one more time. Your misery must be the result of your relationships. It's someone else's job to make you free.

Now, it's important to remember that we *do* need other people and are bound to each other by love, and sometimes even by covenant. But other people cannot do the work of getting us free. We have to do that.

No matter who I talk to, it seems as though most Christians have difficulty with boundaries. We think we can change people, and we think people can change us. With good, godly boundaries, we start to realize that our choices, decisions, and intentions are ours to own and to work on. Part of that work is to ask people for help, to ask people to journey with us. But we have to stop the blame game that keeps us trapped in thinking other people got us in this situation and other people can get us out. I always try to encourage Christians to get the Boundaries series of books by Henry Cloud and John Townsend. They can help us to get to the point where we admit that it was we, not the people around us, who made the decisions that led to our own enslavement.

Recently a beautiful woman I know found herself alone, stuck (again) in a major drug addiction. Her son was removed from her care by the authorities. Her bank account was empty. Fraud charges threatened her with jail time. She was at the end. Her entire family wanted to blame "the guy"—who, to be sure, is a piece of work. A known drug dealer, a terrible influence, a manipulator, I could go on. Without him around, she actually does really well. So it would seem like blaming the guy is the right thing to do. Just kick the guy out and deal with her drug use, and all will be well. Right?

No. Of course not. As tempting as it is to blame the guy, here's a truth I've come to understand very deeply: There will always be another guy. This beautiful young woman could spend the rest of her life cleaning up after the latest guy who messed her up. The real slavery in her is not a particular guy; it's not even just drugs. It's the idea that a guy can fill her life with meaning and purpose. It's that someone else can complete her. This lie is enough to keep on messing with her life until there is nothing left.

The guy is never the answer. Never. Finding freedom for your life is a journey you take with your God and yourself. That journey is deep and hard, but inevitable for the kind of freedom that sets you free.

Who are you blaming for your lack of freedom? Whose fault is it? What can you begin to do right now to take responsibility for your own walk? That kind of truth will set you free.

The Pool of Self-Pity

Poor you. No one has ever had it as bad as you have. No one can even understand the pain of your reality—your memories, the childhood trauma, the abuse, the depth of your own misery, your addiction, your rejection. It goes on and on and on. This litany is difficult to listen to when you've started to recognize the melody of it: It's a loaded lie. It kind of sounds like you are being humble, but really you are narcissistically amazed at your own inability. It's like pride inverted. And it really stinks.

I remember meeting a friend in a small group at my church. She had survived the Rwandan genocide. She was scarred from it, but she had such an incredible freedom story. My friend had witnessed her neighbor chopping her family to death and had fled with her younger brother to the forest to hide with around forty other kids. Some guy who said he was Jesus showed up in the jungle and gave them all food. It kept them alive.

After about forty days and nights in that jungle, the killing stopped and the kids went home. What they saw haunts them still. Dead bodies everywhere. I can't imagine something so terrible. Then she told me about how she was part of rebuilding her neighborhood. She worked with teams of people to bury the dead, to wash the streets, to clean her house, to go to church.

I stopped her. "Go to church?"

"Of course," she said. "We needed God more than ever before. Where else would we go?"

Good point. She said she chose to forgive because she understood that she had been forgiven. And that Jesus told her that to be free meant to forgive. So she forgave. She forgave her neighbors who had massacred her family.

I was speechless. See, I had worked for a long time with a people group who had been systemically abused and neglected in Canada. My church was full of First Nations people, and their stories were horror after horror of abuse and neglect. They were filled with pain. Many of them chose to just numb the pain and sit in a pool of self-pity. And part of me wanted to affirm their choice. But after I met my friend from Rwanda, I decided to ask her to share her story with us. She spoke at our little church gathering, and even though she is the quietest, softest-spoken person I have ever met, she held everyone's complete attention. Not one eye could look away. Everyone just sat and listened to a story that was worse than their own. And then they heard her instructions for freedom: Forgive. My friend had found a new way where it looked like there wasn't a way—an exodus out of generational bitterness and violence and pain. You could hear people swallowing the words and the reality dropping into their hearts: There was a possibility of choosing forgiveness over self-pity. It was a crazy Sunday.

That's the journey the Israelites were on. Not just a way out, but a new way to live, a way that works its way back to the original intentions God had for the world.

We must each choose to live a new way in our everyday decisions. That includes deciding to deal with our past, fully and finally. But it also involves a corporate work. As each person in Rwanda deals with the pain and suffering of their lives and chooses to live a different way, rejecting revenge or fear or bitterness, the whole country begins to change. The people together are able to rise up in a new way. This discovery that there is a way out of our pain, brokenness, cycles, and systems is some seriously good news!

Still, each of us has our own pain to process. Our own memories, childhood traumas, difficulties—things we've done and things done to us. And they are hard, emotionally charged, horrible things that have to be dealt with. Pain is pain. But everyone has to deal with it. No one gets to sit in the pool of self-pity and expect to be free.

There are a few indicators to determine whether you're sitting in the pool of self-pity. Do you feel guilty? Stuck? Are you excusing your symptoms of slavery (addiction, eating, self-soothing, self-loathing)? Are you experiencing apathy and indifference and despair? If the answers to those questions are yes, then you are not moving toward freedom—you are moving away from it.

You've got to move out of this cesspool of narcissism disguised as a friend. You've got to get out of it in order to come to the reality: You get to choose what you are going to do about what has happened in your own life.

That's what the Exodus story screams. God gives the Israelites *choices*. Up until he started speaking to Moses and then to the entire people, they felt completely stuck. As do we. But when God gets involved, he activates our impulse toward freedom. He offers us choices. Those are the sacred parts of the Exodus story. God does his part; we do ours. The partnership leads us to a new way to live.

My friend from Rwanda chose to be free. I think she made

the bravest and most difficult choice of all, but she'll tell you herself with a big smile on her face that it was worth it.

The ultimate posture that prepares us for freedom is *humility*, quite simply coming to the end of ourselves. It's knowing our limits, recognizing that we are human beings in need of saving. It's a fundamental honesty with ourselves. But until we get that honest, we get nowhere.

We can see humility in Moses' personal journey, in the Israelites' desert experience. In Pharaoh we don't see humility; we see pride, and we see that pride yield humiliation. Humility and humiliation are different things. Humility is a choice we make to come into agreement with God about who we are. Humiliation is a consequence; when we live without humility, then our actions often result in humiliation. Moses confronted Pharaoh, not with an army or a new weapon of mass destruction. He confronted him with a shepherd's staff. With himself. That is the power of humility: We finally come to the end of ourselves, and God starts something new.

Finding Freedom

Which of the three traps are you most susceptible to?

What or who can help you break out of these traps?

CHAPTER 10

Picking Blackberries and Bushes on Fire

Moses answered God, "But why me? What
makes you think that I could ever go to Pharaoh
and lead the children of Israel out of Egypt?"

"I'll be with you," God said.

EXODUS 3:11-12

So SLAVERY HAPPENS. Often slowly and gradually. It's a slippery slope, and before we know it, the thing we thought would bring us freedom actually locks us in. We hear the lock turn, and we try the door, and to our horror we can't get out. Now what?

Moses got free from Egypt, and then he built a new life. It seems, by all impressions given in the original story, that it was a good one. Shepherding seemed to fit him, like it was in his genes. He hooked up with an incredibly great woman. Actually, commentators on the Exodus story say that he married up, despite popular portrayals such as *The Prince of Egypt* that suggest he settled. But apparently when Moses brought his family to meet the Israelites, they were amazed; the tribe he married into was uptown—his wife's father was the chief. Not a bad future move. It's safe to say that Moses landed on his feet.

The desert made Moses better—in a way. He left Egypt behind him and started a new life. Fair enough. I wonder what else he left behind. Did he pray? Did he remember who he was? They say in recovery circles that if you go on to freedom without digging through your past and sorting things out, you'll hear another door locking behind you soon enough. Another way to a new prison. Fear, insecurity, anxiety, control, facades, religion, the list is endless. True freedom can only come from a confrontation. Avoidance is not a strategy for freedom. It's simply a holding cell for cowards.

I had a friend who got out of prostitution without acknowledging the pain of her journey. She believed the hype that prostitution was simply her choice and her right. She exercised it when she had to, and then she got out. Full stop. Nothing more to talk about. But it isn't true. Slavery leaves marks. Oppression produces pain. And stuffing that pain down, avoiding that reality—well, that'll kill you. From the inside out.

I never challenged my friend; I just prayed for her. Then one day she had this incredible vision of Jesus during a prayer time. It was of Jesus as a lion. She had no idea it was Jesus, but I was able to fill her in on what that meant. The God of justice was for her and for everyone like her. He promised to set the prisoners free and to right the wrongs of the world.

God was for her. She needed to hear that—not with her ears, but in her heart.

After that vision, something shifted in her. Something changed. I knew it had changed because she came to my house the next day weeping. She couldn't even talk. All she could do was cry. It was really strange because she never cried. She was strong, confident, and hard. But today she was crying.

Eventually she got some stuff out. She told me about the time she "worked" all night long and got back to the hotel early in the morning and her "boyfriend" took her money and made her sleep on the floor. "He made me sleep on the floor," she kept saying. There are worse stories, of course. That wasn't all he made her do. But something about that deeply impacted me. What was happening was my friend was revisiting her past in order to confront her oppressor. We all have to do that to be free.

The temptation to move on with our lives, to bury the past and just forget about it, is strong. Thankfully God doesn't forget us. He meets us. This is what happens to Moses. Moses isn't all stirred up about anything. He's moved on. He's not worried about slavery or oppression or the latest fashion in Egypt. He's just looking after his sheep. He's loving his wife. He's singing with his father-in-law (that may actually be a scene from *The Prince of Egypt*). Until God finds him. Then something happens. A confrontation.

God quickly reminds Moses that the ground he is standing on is *holy*—"other than," like nothing you can really understand. Nothing can prepare you for who God is. God is different. Where God is present, things shift. God has this way of filling normal spaces with difference. You end up with a confrontation that is itself an invitation to live differently. Every confrontation with God leaves people different. We take off our shoes and find a spot on our knees, because this encounter reminds us of our own inability to make a difference.

Powerlessness leads to willingness, which brings God close. In the New Testament, James puts it like this: "God resists the proud, but gives grace to the humble" (James 4:6, GNT). When we meet God, things happen inside of us. God brings things up. He confronts things in us. God tells Moses that he hears the cry. That's really deep, because Moses knew the Israelites were crying; he simply concluded there was nothing he could do about it. It was too hard, and he had already tried and failed, and so he was moving on with his life. But God wasn't moving on. He can't get over oppression. Not without stopping it. So God shows up. And things start to change.

If Moses learned one thing in the desert, it was humility. No question about it. He was humble. He might have even become a little too humble. If the argument he has with God is any indication, he is still pretty convinced he has no chance of doing anything about the situation. And he's right. It's too hard for him. It's too hard for us, too.

I'm a recovering addict. I hate saying that because I like to try to convince myself that I've got it licked. I want to believe that I'm strong enough and powerful enough in my own strength to overcome addiction. But I'm not.

Part of the process of healing for me has been admitting my powerlessness over alcohol or drugs. It's crazy to an outsider; it seems as though we just keep admitting defeat. I used to believe that admitting I was powerless over alcohol was coming into agreement with "the enemy," who would say we are addicts and there is nothing we can do about it. But now I see it a different way. It's actual honesty. It's humility. It's agreeing with the truth that I've got the scars of oppression in my life and I can't do anything about it. It's admitting that I've tried and failed, over and over again. It's coming to the end of myself.

That's the point when I can respond to God, who has the power I need to overcome. It's a submission that's rooted in truth.

Sometimes it takes years in a desert to get to the place where we agree with the truth about our own powerlessness. When we do finally admit it, it is not defeat—it is the opposite of defeat. It's an invitation.

With humility comes grace. With grace comes the presence of God. With the presence of God comes power—the power to overcome, the power to heal, the power to advance, the power to change, the power to shift heaven and earth. God has power. But to access this power requires humility and surrender. Every addict knows this. And every child of God should know this too.

Admitting defeat is the first step. Humility. I can't do it.

I'm powerless over oppression. But I believe God is here. This is where the burning bush comes in. It's God meeting Moses right where he is, reminding him that it's not too late and it's not too hard. God reminds Moses that he cannot settle into a life that's less than his calling. He can run, but he can't hide! God asks Moses to take off his shoes so he can reveal his humanity and get reacquainted with the God who is always present.

I wonder if part of why Moses needed God to show up with an invitation was because of his own guilt over what he had done—his murder of an Egyptian, even his abandonment of his people. It's interesting that God doesn't bring it up. What God does bring up is Moses' humanity. God demands humility from Moses. Perhaps this is how God brings up our sins—he burns them with his presence.

There is no awkward history or strange silence with God. There is with us, of course. Moses has a background of oppression. He most likely compromised his own background and beliefs in the palace. That's got to be difficult to live with. He messed up and actually murdered someone. That's hard to swallow. Then he had to make a run for it. Buried all of Egypt and Israel in the desert and moved on with his life. There is a lot happening on the inside of Moses at the burning bush. Trust me. When Moses took off his sandals, I think a lot of dirt came out.

I read that burning bushes happen all the time in the desert. It's not uncommon in the heat of the desert for a bush to catch fire. What was uncommon in this instance was that the bush never burned up. So Moses went to see. This is the encounter that changes something in Moses. It's when Moses encounters God. A burning bush. In a desert. But it doesn't burn up.

Right from the beginning God uses natural things in a supernatural way. It's kind of his thing. He's been doing it all the time, but sometimes we forget. We expect fire to fall from heaven and consume the bush and shake the earth and for Moses to be transformed from a shepherd to a super-hero and change the world that way. But instead, God comes gently, naturally almost. He comes in a still small voice. A burning bush in a desert of burning bushes. But this one was different.

Of course the symbolism would not be lost on an Israelite. When God sealed the covenant with Abraham that his off-spring would be blessed in order to bring blessing to the entire earth, he passed through Abraham's sacrifices in the form of "a smoking firepot with a blazing torch" (Genesis 15:17, NIV). The smoke from the burning bush might have reminded Moses of this, if he hadn't completely forgotten about the larger story of his people.

A burning bush in a desert. Right where Moses found himself. Far from Egypt. That's the thing about God: When he says he's with us, he's not speaking figuratively. He really is with us—right where we are. And on that day in that desert Moses notices. That might be the real miracle. Moses notices that something is different about that bush. An eternal flame. Something about what he witnesses makes him curious. He follows the whisper to find out more. And in the seeking, Moses finds his heart's desire, his people's hope, his life's calling, and his true friend. He finds God.

I often wonder how many times we miss God because we keep expecting the supernatural signs instead of the natural wonders all around us. Years ago I felt called to plant a church in a very depressing place. It was a concrete jungle of oppression. I was walking on the sidewalk as I set out to survey the land when I saw it. Between the cracks of the sidewalk there was a flower. It was beautiful. Everything was concrete, but that little flower grew right through it. The concrete could not stop life from coming.

I felt something happen in me that day. I went over to the flower. I took a picture. I thanked God for the reminder that he planted and grew life and that no amount of human construction could stop the inevitable spring of his Kingdom. He was coming to this world if he had to push his way through concrete. But he was coming. I felt hope. It was such a small experience—I wish it had been a meteor that fell from the sky and left a massive hole in the earth and everyone in the neighborhood repented and I was able to call it a day and move on. That's not what it was. But it shifted something in me. I noticed it. And I went over. And something shifted in me, something grew in me. Hope.

That image is now tattooed on my arm so I never forget. One of the first people I met in that neighborhood, seemingly a hopeless case at the time, was named Flower. I hoped for Flower because God had planted hope in me. A normal day. A normal me. A normal flower. On fire.

> *Earth's crammed with heaven,*
> *And every common bush afire with God;*
> *But only he who sees, takes off his shoes—*
> *The rest sit round it and pluck blackberries.*
>
> ELIZABETH BARRETT BROWNING

Finding Freedom

How might God be trying to get your attention?

Have you been looking for a big sign?

Is there a whisper you should be listening for?

CHAPTER 11

What's in Your Hand?

Moses objected, "They won't trust me. They
won't listen to a word I say. They're going
to say, 'GOD? Appear to him? Hardly!'"
So GOD said, "What's that in your hand?"
"A staff."

EXODUS 4:1-2

YEARS AGO MY family moved to a very poor and drug-addicted neighborhood. The place we first stepped on to pray about the possibility of a church plant was the place we thought we should begin. It was a dark, horrible park in the center of the area, nicknamed (appropriately) "Needle Park." That park, intended to be an oasis in a concrete jungle, had been taken over by dealers and users. It had become a scary, forbidding, violent place. It was the obvious choice.

We prayed about how to begin our ministry. What was the most strategic way forward? As we prayed, I kept getting the impulse to go hang out in the park. Like it was a normal park.

Eventually we went for it. My friend Rob brought his guitar, I brought a picnic blanket and my two-month-old son, and we went to the park. To hang out. We walked into the middle of Needle Park like a little family on a picnic. It was hilarious. Everyone looked at us like we had lost our minds. Like we were very, very lost. Rob spread out the picnic blanket, and we both sat down. I held my baby on my lap as Rob started to sing.

Insanity, right? Well, it felt like it. People stared at us in dumbfounded wonder. Rob leaned over to me and whispered, "Is this the strategy?" I simply nodded.

Shortly after we sat down, a one-armed man came over to the blanket and introduced himself. His name was Bandit. Not even joking. He asked us what we were doing. We told him we had recently moved to the neighborhood and were looking for friends—simply hanging out in the park. He told us to count him among our friends, and he sat down with us to hang out. Soon another person came, and another. Our picnic blanket was a magnet for people who needed friends.

Several months later we started an initiative every week. Our faith community started to bring our kids to the park to play. We did a needle sweep, wiped down some of the equipment, and then just let our kids be kids in Needle Park. It was like nothing we had ever seen before. As the kids started to play, everyone else stopped what they were doing and just stared at them. The drug dealing stopped. The using stopped. The swearing stopped. Everyone just stared at the kids.

The kids were oblivious. They simply were being

themselves—playing, screaming with delight, using slides and swings that had been unused for a very long time.

Now, let me fast-forward to my last visit to that neighborhood, almost fourteen years later. I was walking right through the middle of the area and had to cross Needle Park to get to the house I was headed to. I saw it first from a distance. There were blossoming lilac trees lining the walkway (there was a walkway!) through the park. A brand-new play area, sparkling clean, with kids playing on it. A community center in the middle of the park, offering games, lunch, and some organized recreation. You know what wasn't there? Drug dealing. Needles. The darkness has left the park. Light has made its home there now. How did that happen?

Well, it happened because we took what we had and who we were, and we offered it to God to use for his purposes. It was an example of the incredible plan God has to use what we have and who we are to confront powers of darkness with the values of God's Kingdom.

This never ceases to amaze me. The strategy God chooses to use every time he invites us into a confrontation with a bully is whatever we have. Yes. That's exactly right. Moses freaks out a bit when God makes it clear that he is inviting Moses to confront Pharaoh and lead his people to freedom. Moses is obviously underqualified for the job. Far from a mighty warrior, Moses is a humble shepherd. He finally gets to the details of the plan: "How will this happen?" he asks (see Exodus 3).

God simply responds with one question. *The* question.

The only one that matters in this situation. "What's in your hand?" (see Exodus 4).

What Moses has in his hand is a stick. A shepherd's staff. I can imagine Moses saying, "All the shepherds have one!" And all throughout the story of the liberation of God's people, you will see this stick. Because what God uses at the start is what he uses at the end; he uses what we have so he can use *us*. God invites Moses to use the stick to liberate his people.

I used to think it was just about the stick. And to be sure, it's a lot about the stick. But there's more going on here. Later on, Jesus demonstrates the prominence of God's question to Moses over and over again, most obviously at the feeding of five thousand hungry people. He tells the disciples that they should feed the crowd, and the disciples start freaking out. Freaking out seems to be the basic response to God's invitation into supernatural living, so if you are prone to freak out, take comfort.

Anyway, the disciples list the obvious obstacles to the task: We don't have enough money, there is not a store nearby, and so on. Jesus then asks them what they *do* have. Sound familiar? Okay. So you don't feel prepared. You aren't ready. You lack qualifications. But what do you *have*? Let's start with this.

This is where it's not just about what you have but who you are. See, Moses is a shepherd. Which is what the Israelites were when they first went to Egypt. And Egyptians despised shepherds. They thought of them as backward and the work as dirty. Shepherding didn't pay well and wasn't very glorious;

the Egyptians were into bigger and better things like industry, buildings, and glory. So when God asks Moses what he has and Moses responds with the stick—it's not just about the stick.

God is asking Moses to go confront Pharaoh with himself. As he is. He does not need to be someone else. He does not need to impress Pharaoh. He simply needs to start with who he is and what he has, and then let God take care of the details.

I cannot tell you how many stories I have that use this recipe.

A thriving brothel chaplaincy network in Australia started with an old lady who baked some cupcakes. It's true. My friend Jan was sixty-six at the time. A retired Baptist elder, she was living in a nice suburb and attending a nice Baptist church in Melbourne. I was the social justice director for The Salvation Army in Australia at the time, and I was trying to figure out a way we could impact the women caught in trafficking and exploitation in the legalized brothels of Australia. Jan's daughter was a good friend of mine. I got a call from Jan to meet up for a cup of coffee and found myself hearing her dilemma.

Jan's phone number was only two digits different from the phone number of the brothel in her neighborhood. She kept getting these awkward calls when people mixed up the numbers. It was disturbing to her and her husband, and Jan was considering changing her phone number. But on the day she was planning to make the change, she felt the Lord speaking to her as she was reading her Bible. She felt a challenge: "Why are you changing your number, Jan?" She told God about her discomfort with the situation and the calls she was getting. And she felt the Lord telling her not to avoid it but to do something about it.

So she called me. We were in the middle of talking about her situation when she asked the golden question: "What should I do?" Now, in the interest of full disclosure, I had no idea what she should do. Seriously. No idea. But I started to brainstorm with her about what she would normally do if a neighbor were in trouble or had just moved in. She responded that it was normal for her to take over some cupcakes and introduce herself, asking how she could help.

That's when it struck me: Let's just be normal. What if we just did the most normal thing?

So, I told Jan, that was the strategy. She would bake cupcakes, and we would go introduce ourselves. Just like we would normally do.

Thankfully Jan believed that was a good strategy. We met on a Tuesday morning and prayed together before we went and knocked on the brothel door. She told me that she had sensed over the weekend that she should be the one who knocked on the door. I was a little offended and responded, "But I'm the professional!"

Jan responded, "I'm the neighbor."

Now, hear this. In the Kingdom of God, neighbor trumps professional *every time*. This escapes us in our formal and professional ministry responses, but it's so important to revisit.

Jesus suggested that the greatest impact for God's Kingdom in our desperate world would happen when we loved God and then simply loved our neighbor. That's not complicated.

Anyway, back to our story. We walked to the brothel and Jan, armed with cupcakes, went up the steps and knocked at the door. One of the brothel managers came to the door to ask what she wanted (Jan is not the normal clientele). Jan was so nervous, she simply shoved the cupcakes forward and said, "I brought cupcakes!"

That's when I saw it. In my own mind I saw the most evil demonic spirit of sexual exploitation over Australia shrink back and shriek, "No! Not the cupcakes!" Because what happened next was inexplicable. The manager of the brothel invited Jan inside to meet the women; Jan was able to tell them that she was a neighbor who saw them and wanted to get to know them. It was unbelievable. Jan exited that brothel about ten feet off the ground. And I went back to The Salvation Army headquarters and called ten of my craziest Salvation Army friends and told them, "Quick! We've got to get busy or the Baptists are going to beat us to the brothels!"

Fast-forward with me. This time about eight years. There is now a network of brothel visitation teams across the nation of Australia. Armed with cupcakes, they bring relationship and connection and hope and the possibility of freedom with them every week to women trapped in prostitution. God has never and is not now looking for amazingly gifted people with advanced weapons systems or schemes of brilliance that will baffle the world. He is looking for shepherds with staffs to confront superpowers not with their amazing courage or ability but with the simple idea that it must be God with and in us that can use us. It's a partnership of eternal significance, power, and consequence.

Who are you? Start there. What's in your hand?

Finding Freedom

What's in your hand?

What does God want you to do with it?

CHAPTER 12

Confrontation

GOD said to Moses, "Go to Pharaoh
and tell him, 'GOD's Message: Release
my people so they can worship me.'"

EXODUS 8:1

I'M A CANADIAN. That means that in my makeup is a cultural norm, a highly valued thing I possess, that inclines me toward niceness. Seriously. I'm not built for confrontation. Canadians typically believe that tolerance is a virtue, and they define *tolerance* as not disagreeing. Of course, true tolerance is disagreeing respectfully, but somehow in my Canadian blood there runs the idea that to disagree is inherently to be unkind.

Confrontation is hard for a lot of people, it turns out. And yet confrontation is key to freedom. Without a confrontation of oppression, there is no freedom.

That's why Martin Luther King Jr. used to go to prison

instead of paying a fine. He did not like prison food, and he really didn't have time to be locked up. He also had plenty of nice benefactors willing to pay his fines and bail him out. He refused it. Why? Because he wanted the confrontation to be clear. He wanted to expose the injustice, to call out the oppressor. He needed a confrontation in order to make freedom possible for his people. As he wrote from Birmingham Jail, "Injustice must be exposed, with all the tension its exposure creates, to the light of human conscience and the air of national opinion before it can be cured."

Now, imagine Moses marching up to the gates of Pharaoh's palace and commanding Pharaoh to let his people go. It was an exercise in insanity. Nowhere in Scripture does it suggest Moses even made an appointment. This was a staged confrontation with the dominant oppressive power. He was creating a confrontation that would lead to an exposure of the oppression that was keeping his people enslaved. Without confrontation, there is no freedom.

The Scripture says that God knew Pharaoh would not let the Israelites go so he "hardened his heart" (Exodus 10:1, NIV) and then proceeded to expose the injustice of Pharaoh's systemic oppression of the Israelites.

Later on in the New Testament, Paul talks about the confrontation of principalities and powers (Ephesians 6:10-17). We are not waging war on people but on spiritual realms. And our war isn't just a super-spiritual esoteric battle. It's a war of ideas, values, and systems that perpetuate real oppression and pain. It's a war on tyranny and truancy and slavery.

It exposes and then overthrows systems and structures that are inherently evil.

The signs that accompany Moses' confrontations are all about this. They expose Pharaoh for the sham that he is, giving evidence of the lack of power he really has. Every single plague is an overthrow of an Egyptian god. It's a confrontation of power systems. It's a battle of values, a spectacular display of God's glory as he takes charge of nature, overthrows corruption, and establishes his authority on the earth. Everyone is surprised; eventually Pharaoh goes from being seen as the incarnation of the sun god to being exposed as a pathetic father who cannot even save his own son.

What tends to happen, instead of confrontation, is compromise. People tend to buckle under the pressure and make a deal with the enemy, a compromise that leaves them not as oppressed as they once were, though still oppressed.

I remember the day I first read about the end of extreme poverty. Jeffrey Sachs, in his book *The End of Poverty*, demonstrates systematically that there is no need for extreme poverty to rage on. It can be met and defeated—if the world will simply confront the power of poverty's grip. He outlines the way it could happen in real life.

In the middle of that book, the revelation hit me hard: We could end extreme poverty in *my lifetime*. As I thought about that possibility, I was filled with joy. But at the same time I was filled with sadness, because I realized that I had come to accept the concept, the idea, the system of extreme poverty. It dawned on me that I had somehow become completely content with little children dying of malnutrition as "normal." This is the subtlety of oppression: I gave into the principalities and powers of extreme poverty by simply agreeing with it in my mind. The poverty of millions upon millions of people had become normal to me.

It's not. If you pay any attention at all to what death by starvation is like, you will soon understand it to be demonic. There is nothing normal about it.

I watched an amazing man accept a Nobel prize for peace. Muhammad Yunus is the founder of the Grameen Bank in Bangladesh; he basically invented microloans for the poorest of the poor. You can read more about his amazing life and story in his book *Banker to the Poor,* but suffice it to say that when he accepted his Nobel prize, he said he was waiting for the day when children would need to visit a museum to learn what extreme poverty used to look like.

Just let that sink in. Muhammad Yunus truly believes the end of poverty is possible; he has lived a life that confronted extreme poverty. As he spoke, I felt the principality of extreme poverty loosen its hold on me.

I had allowed the dominant view of poverty as normal to direct my thoughts and my actions. I had allowed it to go unhindered in my everyday life. But warriors like Muhammad Yunus confronted it. They, like Moses, marched into the arena where extreme poverty had its rule and called it out. And I felt the repercussions in my own life. You can't have freedom without a fight. In order to come into agreement with freedom, you have to come out of agreement with oppression.

There are other oppressions that need confronting. Anxiety, for instance, doesn't have to rule your life. I'm not making the case for some kind of name-it-and-claim-it faith-healing mumbo jumbo. I'm saying that you have to put anxiety in its proper place: under the sovereignty of God.

I have a wonderful friend, an incredibly faith-filled and Spirit-infused leader, who suffers from anxiety. These are things that can go together. She has figured out how to manage her symptoms and her life in such a way that anxiety is no longer the boss of her. To get there she had to confront her anxiety—to expose it for the oppression that it was and then ask God to dethrone it. She had to stop being afraid of being "the person with anxiety." She dragged that monster out into the light. She came out of agreement with it. And she asked God to replace the fear with his kindness, direction, and leadership. She now uses prayer, sacred spaces, personal reflection, and well-scheduled time to help her manage anxiety. But she no longer lives under the fearful oppression that she will never be able to live a full life. She no longer lives with the fear that people might find out she's human and not superhuman. She made a long walk to freedom and it all began when she decided to stop letting anxiety rule her life.

There is a perfectly wonderful explanation for what starts and ends the freedom of the Israelites. It's worship. Why? Well, worship is a way of putting God at the center of our space and time. It's about putting him first. Worship is about recognizing his authority over all others. You always serve what you worship.

The conversations God has with Moses, Moses has with Pharaoh, and then all the people have with God are all about worship. Moses' journey begins with worship, as he removes his shoes and kneels at the burning bush before the presence of Almighty God. Worship is what Moses confronts Pharaoh with as he conveys God's message: "Let my people go, *so that they may worship me*" (Exodus 8:1, NIV, emphasis added). Worship happens at the end of the journey out of Egypt, with the shake of a tambourine and the bursting out in celebratory song, as Miriam leads the people in dancing and rejoicing because God is who he says he is (Exodus 15:20-21).

Worship realigns us with who is in charge. I remember someone once saying, during a time of sung worship, that sometimes you sing because you believe and sometimes you sing until you believe—and both are good. That's because worship shifts things. Worship is warfare—a confrontation of spiritual power, realigning us with truth.

Confrontation always precedes freedom. There is no getting free without a confrontation. That's actually why many wars are fought. Eventually the distress of the current situation creates a crisis, and that crisis turns into a confrontation, and that's when freedom has the potential to emerge. This is always the case, whether it's an external confrontation or an internal one.

Any counselor will tell you that you will never be free in any area of your life that you aren't willing to confront. Do it now. Be honest now. Deal with the issues now. Bring the darkness into the light now.

Years ago I talked to a woman who changed an entire nation's mind about the oppression of sexual exploitation. I've heard people talk about prostitution as the "oldest profession," but she calls it the oldest *oppression*. And she's right. When she commissioned a study on the realities of prostitution, it became very clear the kind of oppression it was. It was a slave master that kept women—mostly poor, uneducated ethnic minorities—in absolute hell. So she set about changing the nation's mind, educating the nation's children and leaders, and confronting the power of sexual exploitation. She made some amazing progress. Last I checked, her nation had decreased street prostitution by over 60 percent in only ten years. When I asked her how she did it, she gave me two keys.

First, she told me, you've got to imagine a better world.

Second, you've got to truly understand the oppression.

Worship helps us imagine a better world. It is, perhaps, what worship is designed to do. It allows us to lift our gaze upward and imagine the world from the cosmic view of God, on a throne, filled with kindness, forgiveness, and grace. It enables us to see him ready to bring justice and freedom and hope and release to captives. It instructs us to proclaim good news to the excluded. The longer we worship God, the more we can imagine a better world. As we imagine that better world, a world where everyone was created to be free, we will begin to really understand oppression.

Moses gets insight and strategy in worship. He confronts Pharaoh believing that God intends freedom for people, and Pharaoh is gradually revealed for the tyrant toddler that he is. The confrontation leads to light, and light leads to revelation, and revelation leads to freedom. And freedom is what this whole thing is all about.

Finding Freedom

What oppression have you come to agree with?

Can you come into agreement with God's perspective on that situation?

Are you willing to confront the enemy of your freedom? It's time to believe that freedom is truly possible in your life.

CHAPTER 13

Don't Be Afraid

Moses spoke to the people: "Don't be afraid. Stand firm and watch GOD do his work of salvation for you today."

EXODUS 14:13

I REMEMBER THE day it happened. I had been clean and sober and out of jail for a while, but I was bored. I felt like nothing mattered. I was so tired and weary, and I felt isolated and alone. I walked the familiar streets of a Toronto neighborhood, in the general direction of where I could score. I really just wanted the feeling of uselessness to leave.

On my way I noticed the open door of a little Salvation Army church on the corner. There were people inside. It was a Sunday night, in the middle of a service. I slipped into the back row thinking I'd delay the inevitable.

What happened next was stunning. I had walked into the middle of a "testimony time," the time in a service where anyone can just stand up and tell of something God had done that week. As soon as I sat down, an old blind lady stood up to testify. She shared that a young girl for whom she had been praying for many years had recently come into relationship with God. She asked everyone in that meeting place that night to continue to pray for her as she tried to turn her life around. And then she said, "Her name is Danielle. Will you join me?"

I was amazed. I was awed. I was filled with a holy kind of fear—the kind of respect that makes you remember just how big God is, how much bigger his plans are than you. I realized on the spot that I wasn't alone. I would never be alone. God was with me. And he had people everywhere. It was a sign.

God invades the everyday, ordinary drudgery of life with his presence. He did it for Moses, with a bush in a desert and God's presence awakening him to his true purpose. He did it next for the Israelites and even for the Egyptians as he poured out his sovereign hand to display his power. He does it still in our world all the time.

God's signs are not for themselves; they serve a purpose— have you listened to them lately?

The overarching theme in all of God's signs is very clear to those of us who have been delivered from oppression: Do not be afraid. See, fear is the currency of oppression. To confront oppression is to confront fear.

I always understood that fear was a driving force in how power oppresses. Fear is what keeps people quiet when wrong things happen. Fear is what allows people to keep bowing under pressure. Fear is instilled in oppressed people to get them to submit to the oppression. It's how so many oppressors can govern and oppress people who outnumber them. The Israelites were afraid of Pharaoh, and that fear kept them under his control. I knew that. What I didn't know—and this information would change the way I think of oppression forever—is that Pharaoh was afraid of the Israelites.

Make no mistake. Both the oppressed and the oppressor are participating in the same fear. If you participate in fear, you will either oppress or you will be oppressed. Give it some thought and study. Every despot, every oppressive leader in the world, was terrified. Hitler used at least seven cars as decoys and never slept in the same place twice. He was terrified, and he terrorized people as a result. Stalin used to randomly kill his senior officers because he was afraid they were going to try to kill him. On and on it goes. Terrified leaders oppress terrified people.

Is it any wonder that whenever God encounters his people, he leads with, "Do not be afraid"? He says this 365 times in the Bible—like we need to be reminded every day.

Our world is saturated with fear. We are told to fear people we don't know. We are convinced that our neighbors are potential threats. We lock ourselves inside of our homes, becoming prisoners in a small world of our own making. We look suspiciously at anyone who doesn't belong. We are so afraid. And our fear leads to oppression. One way or another.

So what do we do? This is where God's remedy is so beautiful.

Years ago I was journeying with a friend of mine, Stepfanie. She was getting untangled from a life of oppression. She had been exploited by a terrible bully, a pimp who had done horrible things to her, oppressing her in almost every way a person can be oppressed. She was still terrified when she thought of him. Even though she was now in a safe place, she still had nightmares and times when he would come into her mind and bully her still.

One time we were praying together, and the bully showed up in her prayers. She shut down; she said she didn't want to keep praying. The bully was tormenting her, reminding her of all that he would do to her when she returned. We stopped for a bit to take a break. And then I got mad. I got mad at the bully. I got mad at the injustice of it all. This tyrant had already taken too much of my friend's life. So I proposed to Stepfanie that we go back to that moment in prayer where he showed up. We weren't going to ignore it or evade it or pretend it didn't happen. We certainly were not going to agree with him, and we weren't going to give him our prayer time. We would confront the bully.

But not by ourselves. Oppressors are too big for us. I suggested that we invite Jesus to come right into the place where the bully was. Rather than us confront the bully in our weakness and fear, we invited Jesus to reveal where he was in the midst of the confrontation.

Stepfanie agreed to do it because she is strong and was

choosing not to let fear dominate her life. So we prayed again, and we invited Jesus to show his presence.

Stepfanie began to laugh. I remember being confused. "What's going on?" I asked.

She looked at me with this big goofy grin and said, "Well, he showed up!"

I sighed a breath of relief. Sometimes we have to remind ourselves that Jesus is real. I asked her where he was, and that's when she explained what was so funny. Jesus had shown up right where I had hoped he would—between her and the bully. But that wasn't what was so funny. Jesus, Stepfanie said, had shown up so huge that she had to hug his left calf to withstand his presence. "He was bigger than I expected," she said with a huge grin. "Way bigger than *he* expected as well!" She described with joy and freedom what it felt like to watch this bully, this oppressor, literally run away from Jesus in her prayer.

The key to fighting fear is not avoiding it or stopping the confrontation. It is not to pretend you are stronger than you are. It's not thinking your way or shaming your way out of fear. I meet so many people who think that if they pretend they aren't afraid, they won't be. Or they are so ashamed to admit they are afraid that they cover it up with false bravery. That will never work. The only thing that can drive out fear, the Bible tells us, is perfect love (1 John 4:18). In the Exodus story, that perfect love comes with the presence of God. It is God who drives out fear.

When Moses asks God how he's going to lead the people

of God to freedom, God responds, "I'll be with you" (Exodus 3:12). And he means it. God's presence starts to erode fear. As Moses rediscovers the character and presence of God, fear begins to loosen its grip, and faith begins to grow.

I heard recently that all of us are living in either faith or fear. I didn't like it when I heard it. It struck a nerve, I think. But if you think of faith at one end of a continuum and fear at the other, you have to walk in one direction or the other. There is no way to walk in them both.

When Pharaoh hardened his heart and tightened his grip of oppression on the Israelites, this was no doubt Moses' worst fear realized. Moses called on God and God showed up, bringing judgment against Pharaoh. Each of the signs that followed confronted one of Egypt's gods, idols that the Egyptians used to keep people afraid. God showed up, and he was bigger than they expected. God's presence dwarfed Egypt's systems of power and control.

It gets better. The sign of God's presence is not just judgment of the enemy; it's an expression of support of his people. This is true throughout the Exodus story. When Pharaoh released Israel and then changed his mind, chasing them to the edge of the Red Sea, God showed up, making a way for Israel to continue their exodus and bringing a final judgment on the oppression of Egypt. When the people were worried about what they were going to eat, Moses asked God to show up, and God provided food for them from the sky. Literally. From the sky. When the people didn't know where to go, God came like a cloud in the day and a pillar of fire in the night so they could follow him and not get lost in the desert. I think you are getting the idea. God's presence is the key to banishing fear from our lives.

Finding Freedom

What are you afraid of?

What other people think? Insignificance? Failure? Weakness? Risk?

Why don't you try going to those places, in your prayers or your thoughts or in real life, and inviting God's presence into those spaces. Let him show up right where your fear is. Let perfect love drive fear out. You will encounter the sign of God's presence and power as you invite him in. Trust me: He'll be much bigger than you were expecting.

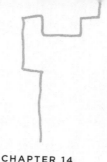

CHAPTER 14

Start Now and with You

Now, if we can only keep a firm grip on
this bold confidence, we're the house!
That's why the Holy Spirit says,
"Today, please listen;
don't turn a deaf ear as in 'the bitter uprising,'
that time of wilderness testing!
Even though they watched me at work for forty years,
your ancestors refused to let me do it my way;
over and over they tried my patience.
And I was provoked, oh, so provoked!
I said, 'They'll never keep their minds on God;
they refuse to walk down my road.'
Exasperated, I vowed,
'They'll never get where they're going,
never be able to sit down and rest.'"

HEBREWS 3:6-11

I THINK THE opposite of standing is sitting. Maybe it's lying down? Obviously it's reclining in some position other than vertical. I was praying the other day with a friend who struggles with what I (and most of the people I know) also struggle with: procrastination. We were praying through the classic Psalm 23 ("The Lord is my shepherd"), and it struck us that the context of the verse that talks about the valley of the shadow of death is *movement*. The psalmist is *passing through* the valley; even in the midst of our enemies, the Lord is preparing a feast for us. The movement of the psalm suggests that we move through even our darkest times. We don't lie down in the valley; we walk through it. We sit at the table God sets in the presence of our enemies, enjoy his feast, and then get up and keep moving. The enemy never has the final word. We move on.

Then I had a flash to a Scripture that I turn to a lot for comfort: We can rest in the shadow of the Almighty (Psalm 91). The image is of a bird that covers its chicks under its wings, but the context involves restful *movement*, a safe *journey*. There is a shadow we can rest in *in the midst of* the scorching heat of the desert. God offers relief in the midst of a journey.

That got me thinking about God as leading us somewhere. We are following God, and in that process there is a supernatural shifting, an exchange of our worry for his peace, his presence.

Now, hang in there; I'm going to connect the dots. A few weeks ago at an event, my husband shared about a classic invitation from Jesus: "Come to me, all you who are weary and burdened, and I will give you rest." I love that verse. Except my lovely man kept reading: "Take my yoke upon you and learn from me. . . . For my yoke is easy and my burden is light" (Matthew 11:28-30, NIV).

What? What does a yoke (think oxen working in a field) have to do with rest?

The people of God had to *fight* for their rest. The Promised Land had to be *conquered*. When they arrived at this land of rest, for the first time in a generation they had to grow their own food. For the people of God, rest involved *movement*.

Salvation, as it is talked about in Scripture, always involves movement. It is a way to walk, a place to enter, a new way to live.

We tend to think of salvation as a one-time, miraculous event. A static thing that happened to us. No further movement.

Consider how the culture around us might recast what Jesus says in Matthew 11: "Feeling tired? Try doing nothing today. Watch some TV and hang out." Maybe it's just me, but have you ever felt better after a day like that? We've believed the world about how to solve our fatigue—which is a bit weird, considering almost half of North Americans are struggling with depression.

Now, don't get me wrong. Having a day off is a fine idea—especially if it involves time for refreshing your soul. One of the Ten Commandments God gave the Israelites is a regular Sabbath, which was meant to create a rhythm of refreshment.

But we have bought the lie that a life of laziness, or of mindless entertainment and activities, will give us rest. They don't. Feed laziness and you breed more. Feed lonely bitterness and you get even more lonely. We reap what we sow.

So, what am I saying? Get up. Stand up. Right now. Do something. Write. Dream. Play. Go for a long walk in a beautiful place. Take your kids on a wagon ride. Go to the gym. Read your Bible. Pray (try on your knees just for fun). Don't lie down. Don't do it. Stand up. The Scriptures tell us to be prepared; there is an enemy who roars around, "looking for someone to devour" (1 Peter 5:8, NIV). So, says Paul, take a stand against the enemy. Get up. Get ready for a fight. Get prepared for a battle (1 Corinthians 16:13). Fight for your rest—real rest, the spiritually filled kind. Add a whole night of prayer to your already packed schedule. I dare you. When Jesus was overwhelmed, that's what he did (Luke 6:12). Find a posture of rest that commits to changing the world. I'm literally humming the classic song "I get knocked down, but I get up again; you are never gonna keep me down" as I write this.

Many of us have had our hits. And the enemy hits hard. But we have got to keep moving. This is a battle. We are in a war. Salvation isn't a prayer I put in my pocket and hope it works when I'm in trouble. It's a new way to live. So live it. Stand up and walk out what you already know. Live what you've already learned. Stop learning more until you've actually implemented what you already know. Stand up. Get ready. Go.

Jay Leno once said he'd do anything for the perfect body. Except diet and exercise. That's why I stopped listening to my body. I recently received a five-day free pass to an Ultimate Fighting Championship (UFC) gym. It's not the normal, "come as you are" sort of affair. Contrary to the gym I currently belong to, which offers a "judgment-free atmosphere" with massage beds for after your workout, the UFC gym is a little . . . well, what shall we call it?—hyper. It's a hard-core, intensely pressurized, macho muscle place that makes you feel both inspired and afraid at the same time. You can almost smell the testosterone.

Now, I've dabbled in many different athletic ventures over the years. I've played and coached basketball, I did the marathon thing for many years, ventured into cross-training for triathlons, and most recently dabbled with yoga. (Don't worry, I kept my third eye completely shut!) Then I took a break from pushing myself, taking some time to rest and "listen to my body." This was recommended to me as a way of working on other areas of my life (like my emotions and, well, listening to my body). Now, I want to be clear that embracing a calmer spirit was an excellent exercise for me. But it turns out my body *never* wants to do anything.

Well, that's not entirely true. It wants to eat. A lot. Mostly salty carbs and a whole lot of sugar. Other than that, though, my body is a complete slacker. A total liar. To be very honest, if I were to listen to my body, I'd be watching Netflix and eating chips and dip right now.

So I stopped listening to my body. I dove into UFC hyper-land with the free pass in my sweaty little hand and did a five-day "boot camp." I thought I might die. But after the third day (go figure), something shifted. My body kind of woke up. Call it a resurrection if you must. But if you don't believe it was miraculous, then listen to this: On the fourth day I woke up crazy early to fit in an extra workout before my busy day. Very, very early. And I really enjoyed it. It felt good. It got my energy up. It made my quads burn and my brain buzz.

It turns out my body was totally wrong about itself. It was conflicted and selfish. It was, well, lazy. My body, it turns out, is also almost always too tired to pray. Too tired to go help at the church, too tired and exhausted to volunteer. When it comes to exercise (and, well, almost everything else), listening to your body is a bit overrated. My body regularly lies to me.

As the Israelites walked for forty years, waiting to enter the Promised Land, God was teaching them that freedom was not some elusive super-spiritual reality. It was a lifestyle they would have to train for. They were going to have to learn how to stop taking and start sharing. They were going to have to learn, the hard way, how to stay dependent on God instead of seizing control for themselves. They were going to have to learn how to worship God without trying to control him. It was going to be a long process, a journey of not just getting out of Egypt but getting Egypt out of them. It was an inside-out journey—which is the hardest of any journey. You can hardly go a paragraph in the whole Exodus story without the Israelites complaining about what they had to do!

Paul told the Corinthians, "I beat my body and bring it into submission" (1 Corinthians 9:27, WEB). I think I'm grasping what he means. The dynamics of the UFC gym help me to understand the work involved in our freedom.

The Bar Is Set High by Someone Else

Sometimes we need someone else to set the pace. Recently a class instructor told us that we were born able to do certain movements; if we can't do them now, it's because we learned how *not* to do them. As we practiced doing them again, he said, we would uncover the potential we were born with.

Sounds a lot like the Exodus story to me. God was a trainer for the Israelites, helping them learn what they were born to do.

The classes I was taking at the UFC gym were led by trainers. They didn't believe the lies my body was telling me. Let's imagine God as a trainer who knows much more than we do about what we were created to do and be.

Other People Are Doing It Too

When I'm alone, I can easily convince myself that I should back off and take it easy. But when someone is beside me, pressing through pain and pushing a bit harder, well, it's a compelling inspiration.

None of us was made for a solo career. Not even Moses. One of the classic stories in Exodus is when Moses' father-in-law, Jethro, comes to visit and watches Moses leading the people all by himself. He is burning himself out. Jethro takes him aside and explains a bit of human behavior and basic boundaries to him: Get some help (Exodus 18:13-23). Jethro is right. None of us can do this by ourselves. We are called as a community, into a community.

People Are Watching

I know this sounds a bit, well, crass. But it's just true. I can't cheat or quit when others are watching. It's an instant accountability thing.

There is no shortage of stories in the Exodus account where people try to sneak and steal and keep. They are busted over and over again as a form of God's grace. Training people in accountability is part of freedom.

There's a Plan

Some gyms have a lot of machines. I get overwhelmed by the sheer volume and complexity of them. I'm never really sure what I'm doing. It's very demotivating to wander around and try to pick some things that might help.

The bigger picture is so key. An expert workout delivered by an expert trainer is highly motivating. God doesn't always explain his plans to us, but we can rest assured that he has a plan that we fit into. God's plan for the Israelites was to make them a nation that would represent him to the rest of the world. It was way bigger than they could ever comprehend—maybe even still. But the secret to really being trained in this way is to give in to the wisdom and wealth of God's plan. He's got it.

This is not a UFC gym advertisement. I swear. I'm getting nothing from them except pain and sweat. But all of this exercise experimenting has led me to some other conclusions about our bodies and our spirits. See, I've been in spiritual training with this way of life called Infinitum. (Check it out at infinitumlife.com.) It's a lot like a UFC gym, but for the spirit. It has spurred me on to embrace some new disciplines and plans for my spiritual life that I simply would not have done on my own. Someone has set a standard that is higher than the one I might have set for myself. People are with me on the journey; they inspire me to keep trying, keep pushing, keep going. Others are watching. That matters. Finally, there's a plan. I'm not overwhelmed by the sheer volume of discipleship methods. This is simple and yet hard. It hurts a bit but in all the right ways. It awakens me to the possibility of a life that is different from the one I would choose if left to my own devices and desires.

So take this as a free pass to try it out. Give it a shot. Make a plan and start to implement it. Beat your body into submission. Because chances are, it is lying to you too. It's lazy. My flesh is tired of seeking God, but on my knees I'll stay. Want to join me?

Finding Freedom

What are you doing to live in freedom and experience God's rest?

What disciplines can you incorporate into your life to stay active in your pursuit of freedom?

Can you think of a person who could be an accountability partner for getting into spiritual shape?

CHAPTER 15

Living Openhandedly

> GOD said to Moses, "I'm going to
> rain bread down from the skies for
> you. The people will go out and
> gather each day's ration. I'm going
> to test them to see if they'll live
> according to my Teaching or not."
>
> **EXODUS 16:4-5**

THE EXODUS STORY is filled to the brim with lessons in *enough*. Enough is not Egypt's normal. It's not ours either.

Occasionally I feel like I'm in an episode of *Hoarders*. You know, the show that reveals the apartments and houses of people who just keep collecting things and won't throw anything away. I know of several people who sleep on their couches because their beds are completely stacked full of boxes and files and books and instruments and, well, other junk. They can't get into their bedrooms anymore. Experts suggest that this is an actual mental disorder. I'd suggest it's just an extreme version of what most of us suffer from: greed.

Now greed is a bit tricky, because most of us have been

convinced that it's measured by how much stuff we *have*. But in any Western, developed country, even if we are living on our community's minimum wage or on a government subsidy, we are still in the top 10 percent of the wealthiest people on the planet. I'm not kidding. Check out your own status at globalrichlist.com.

Now, just because we're rich, that doesn't mean we are greedy, does it? What does greed look like?

Stuff doesn't necessarily oppress us, but our need for it does. Greed makes a slave of each of us.

My friend was a missionary for a few years in a pretty poor country. On the compound where she lived were several families. Some of them were from in-country and some were from Western countries. One of the young little boys (we'll call him Johnny) received a tricycle from his home country as a gift. He was so excited that he was riding it around the compound all morning. His friend had never seen a tricycle before and was running around after him, enjoying the excitement. Eventually, Johnny got tired of riding, at which point his friend asked him, "Can I try?"

Johnny got very mad and said, "No!" He wouldn't get off the tricycle. There were some swings close by, and Johnny realized that he felt like doing something different. But he didn't want to share his new trike, so he picked it up in his little arms and carried it over to the swing set. He was not going to share that trike!

Greed looks like that. It's a staunch refusal to share. We believe the lie that we won't have enough, and oppression takes root in our hearts. The fear makes us both oppressed by a desire for more—and oppressors in our refusal to share.

If we are honest with ourselves, we are a lot like that little boy with his silly trike. We close our hands around whatever we can get, and we don't let anyone else have it. Actually, we have been taught to do this. A whole generation has been convinced that we are empty and dissatisfied until we have stuff that belongs to us. There's a great video about the conspiracy of marketing and consumerism that convinced us of this lie at storyofstuff.com.

Of course, we know the exact opposite is true—we can live our whole lives with everything we want (stuff) and be just as empty and lonely and lost as with a few dollars a day.

Someone asked Pope John Paul II at the end of his life what was the greatest threat to the next generation. He identified two: excessive capitalism and the death of children not yet born. That's deep. When we make our whole lives about money, wealth, and sales, we end up commodifying everything—even human beings.

I was speaking to a young person the other day. She told me she had an abortion because she couldn't afford a baby. *Did you catch that?* It's a subtle thing but incredibly important: The decision whether to keep a life was based on money. Keeping a baby was subjected to an economic equation. How much is a baby worth?

It's no wonder the sale of human beings is the fastest growing crime on the planet. We've taken greed to a new level, measuring our lives as though people are cash.

The real problem with greed is that it grows. Remember how Mother Teresa answered when asked how she could believe in a God who allows people to go hungry? She replied that poverty exists in the world not because of God but because God's children refuse to share. Ouch. Greed grows like an infection in us, hollowing us out inside, numbing us to other people's needs and plights.

Greed isn't a new idea; it's an old one. The original act that broke our relationship with God and each other was Adam and Eve in the Garden, wanting what they couldn't have. Greed has caused war, famines, dictatorships, and countless casualties of crime.

Jesus always attacked greed with excessive generosity. He lived what I call an openhanded life. He was free. Even salvation is generous—he made it free for anyone who would receive it.

It wasn't that Jesus didn't receive; even as a young baby he accepted extravagant gifts. And it wasn't that Jesus didn't have any money; he appointed a disciple just to look after the cash. It's that Jesus wasn't *owned* by his money, gifts, status, successes. Freely he received, freely he gave. This is an openhanded posture.

Jesus instructs his disciples to make this the posture of their whole lives: "Freely you received, so freely give" (Matthew 10:8, WEB). Once the disciples catch this radical idea of living openhandedly in a closefisted world, it's amazing what happens. Thousands of people saved in one day. Miraculous prison breaks. People are healed, saved, set free.

Dead people are raised up. People start to live together to share resources; the Scriptures tell us that the first disciples so caught this message that in their community no one was in need (Acts 4:32-35). They solved poverty by learning to live openhandedly.

This, by the way, was the miraculous sign for the Israelites in the desert: "The one who gathered much did not have too much, and the one who gathered little did not have too little. Everyone had gathered just as much as they needed" (Exodus 16:18, NIV). Wow. What started as a hard journey for a bunch of Egyptian-oppressed slaves had become a practice of daily freedom by believing God would provide for them and gathering just what they needed. The Exodus story shows us a way out of greed: We see the Israelites delivered from a greedy oppressor who is refusing to live openhandedly with them, even at the prompting and invitation of God himself. But that same oppression is rooted deeply within the Israelites. The desert reveals this oppression in their lives, until God helps the people learn to keep walking into freedom by sharing. Freely they received, now freely they learned to give.

Why don't we live like that? Why don't we know more about this radical way to live? It's like the UFC of greed-fighting, a full assault on the spirit of greed that seeks to bind up an entire culture. How about we introduce ourselves to Jesus' radical generosity as a lifestyle? That could really impact our world.

Ever since I began to see this openhanded posture in the

Scriptures—the way Jesus lived openhandedly—I've been trying to live the same way. It's hard, but it's fun. When my son was a little boy, we went to visit some friends of ours who had already spent some years learning this way of living. They shared their home with others and opened their house for community meals—sharing their food and their family with people who didn't have either. It was an exciting way to live. Our kids were playing in the toy room when we heard a fight break out. "It's mine!" we heard. My friend Aaron rushed into the room and said to his eldest son, "Whose toy is that again?"

The boy looked at his father and said, "It's Jesus' toy."

"That's right," said Aaron. "And Jesus let you play with it, right?"

"Yes," said his young boy.

"So do you think Jesus would mind if you gave it to your friend to play with now?"

"Okay."

Problem solved.

Which way should we raise our children? To carry their trikes around out of fear that another kid may take the pleasure from them? Or to see their things as received and shared, living fearlessly in the face of greed?

One of the root problems of greed is a question of ownership. We think because we bought something or were given something that it belongs to us. What we forget is an essential Kingdom principle: Everything belongs to God. He shares the entire resources of the earth with his people. God has literally

written this into the instructions to the Israelites, by reset-
ting debts every seven years—eliminating the bondage that
comes from debt. He talks about the land being the Lord's and
needing to rest. He makes certain that farmers don't harvest
everything for themselves but leave some grain and produce
behind for those who don't have enough food. God gives the
Israelites a workout manual to learn the values of freedom. All
of these instructions are in the book of Exodus because it is
about freedom.

How rude of us to take what is freely given and hoard it
for ourselves. And not only is it rude, it's also rotten. Like an
episode of *Hoarders*, where people's quality of life is diminished as a result of their closefistedness, we invest our lives
in things that don't matter, and our lives are diminished for
it. I recently watched some footage of riots in a major city.
The majority of clips I saw were not just about destruction;
they were about greed. Everyone, as soon as there was a
chance, was grabbing things—anything they could carry.
TVs, computers, all kinds of things. Just grabbing them
and running. What a great picture of closefisted living. No
concern for others. No concern for the cost involved to the
rest of society. Like toddlers who haven't learned to share,
their actions betrayed an attitude of "It's mine!"

It's time to live another way. It's time to get radical in our
fight against the oppression of greed. It's time to pry open
our tightfisted hands and share what was freely given to us.

Loosening this oppression will take intentional practice.
The *idea* will not change anything. It will need to be an

action program. Let's think through some ideas that could make this real in our everyday lives—a freedom workout, if you will.

Make Sharing an Everyday Thing

Practice giving something away every day. It doesn't have to be huge—even small things—but share them on purpose. It doesn't have to be stuff. Maybe you share your friendship with someone who doesn't deserve it. Maybe you share your lunch with someone who doesn't have one. A sweater. A toy. A music library!

Practice Hospitality

Hospitality is the art of inviting people into our space. It's lost to most of our generation. Having people over to our place is about being openhanded where we hang out. Try to include someone new—someone outside your group of friends.

Remember Your Place in the World on the Wealth Index

Surely you can spare some munchies to literally share your money with those who don't have any. Sponsor a child. Put the child's picture up where others will see it and share the news that we can give so that others can live. Watch the revolution unfold as you live a different way.

Swap Clothing and Stuff

Swapping clothing and other stuff is a great way to combat the excessive need to always be buying. Share stuff. Have friends come on over and bring some of their stuff and have a swap meet. It's really fun and it's free and it's about sharing. I've known of groups of people who do this with toys, too. It makes life much richer and fights the war against "stuff."

Work Together

Get your family or friends together and watch *The Story of Stuff*, then measure your own wealth using the global rich list (globalrichlist.com). Brainstorm about what you can do to combat greed as a lifestyle and live in freedom. Try some stuff and spread the word.

Finding Freedom

What has God provided you with?

Who can you share it with?

CHAPTER 16

Sabbath in Defiance of Slavery

> Observe the Sabbath day, to keep it holy. Work
> six days and do everything you need to do. But
> the seventh day is a Sabbath to GOD, your God.
> Don't do any work—not you, nor your son, nor
> your daughter, nor your servant, nor your maid, nor
> your animals, not even the foreign guest visiting
> in your town. For in six days GOD made Heaven,
> Earth, and sea, and everything in them; he rested
> on the seventh day. Therefore GOD blessed the
> Sabbath day; he set it apart as a holy day.
>
> EXODUS 20:8-11

THERE IS A famous book by a rabbi named Abraham Heschel.
The Sabbath is a little book about the mystical power of the
Sabbath; it has a hushed tone, as though Abraham were writing about something sacred, unveiling a secret artifact and
sharing its dangerous power with the world. When I first
read it, I didn't quite get it. It felt odd.

I thought I should look into the practice of the Sabbath

a bit more. And I discovered that the Sabbath becomes a big deal at the Exodus. We don't hear much about it before that besides the fact that God took a Sabbath. After he was done creating the entire cosmos (and maybe others—who knows for sure?), God rested. But besides it being a part of the rhythm of creation, the Sabbath really isn't a big deal until after the Exodus. Then it becomes a major deal. I mean it's a really, really big deal. The Sabbath comes to the forefront of the meaning of being called God's people. God writes the Sabbath down and calls it holy and tells the people that if they don't practice the Sabbath, then they are not really his people.

Why does it become such a big deal in this story? Why does it take such prominence? What is the big deal?

I'd suggest the Sabbath is a way of defying slavery. Slaves, by definition, cannot stop working. Sabbath is living in such a way that we are no longer slaves.

The Israelites had spent three hundred years or so assimilating into the dominant cultural value system of Egypt. Generations had succumbed to never ceasing from work. It was normal to work all the time. The bustling and ever-increasing economy of Egypt demanded nonstop work. That work was imposed on the Israelites.

That's the definition of slavery. You can't stop working.

God takes a look at this people, stamped with his image but conformed to the image of Egypt. They were supposed to look more like God than Pharaoh. So God sets out to re-create them into the people that deep down they already are.

They need to make a journey from slaves to cocreators with God. From driven to contented. That's when the Sabbath becomes a big deal.

See, the Sabbath is a pattern for creation. It's the way a Creator who isn't constantly anxious, worried, or self-obsessed works. It's about more than him. It's about the entire created order. God is not a control freak obsessed with his own power and glory, not allowing anyone to stop working. He is a creator who creates for pleasure and beauty.

Nothing is beautiful about slavery. It's functional but not personal. That's not the God we find in Genesis or Exodus. The Sabbath is not about function. It's about people.

I remember the day my son asked me to take him to the park and I readily agreed. Then he asked if I was going to bring my phone with me. I said yes. He looked sad. I asked him what the problem was. He told me that when I had my phone, I wasn't really *with* him. It hurt a bit. Like the truth that hurts before it sets you free. I had become enslaved to my phone, and it hurt my relationship with my son. My time with him became another occasion to get some work done rather than simply enjoy his company.

The Sabbath is defiance against function. It really is. It's one day a week where God says, "Don't do any work. Enjoy me. Enjoy food. Enjoy people. Prioritize relationships. Waste time." Even writing these words are counterintuitive to me. The reason? I'm a slave—immersed in a dominant culture that prizes function over relationship and success over beauty and work over freedom. I'm in Egypt. I look more like Egypt than I do Yahweh. And that's a problem, because the one who made me designed me to look like him. I should look like my Father.

Surely that's why the Sabbath is all the rage these days. It's like a rediscovery of our birthright—like a lost treasure buried so long ago that no one knew where to find it. Surely there is a cry to be heard in the oppression of depression, sleeping disorders, and elevated stress levels (of both people and the earth). Surely there's a cry to be heard in cows injected with growth hormones to grow unnaturally fat or fast because none of us can wait a single day or hour or minute for what we want. None of us can stop working—not ever, not even think about it—because we are more inclined toward money and status and success than relationship, beauty, and freedom.

I found myself at an Apple store one Labor Day weekend. In America, Labor Day was created to give workers a break. But on this Labor Day weekend I had something needing repair. I commented that I probably wouldn't be able to get my phone back until the Tuesday after Labor Day. The man looked at me like I had just been born. "We are open on Labor Day."

I remember saying to him, "Do you not get what Labor Day is celebrating?"

He smiled at the sarcasm and said, "I get time and a half."

If you had to choose between a day off once a year or more money, you would pick more money. Of course you would. We live in Egypt.

But when the oppression of work without rest begins to

wear us down and we start to buckle under the weight of "never enough," the sheer weight of the whole world revolving around us, we start to look for some alternative answers. And we don't have to look far. Look at the Sabbath.

The Sabbath suspends time. It points backward and forward at the same time. It grabs holds of the future God has planned—a future of *shalom*. *Shalom* is a Hebrew word often translated as "peace" but meaning a whole lot more. It is about wholeness and right relationships and the valuing and living of goodness. One scholar says it's about the space between everything being made right. Think about that. The space between everything. Like the way you relate to others and the way they relate to you. The way you think about yourself and the way others think about you. The holes in your life that your serenity slips through (doubt, fear, anxiety, depression), all being filled up with goodness and peace.

Shalom is the primary part of the Sabbath. When Jewish people celebrate Sabbath by sitting around a dinner table with the family and relishing the freedom and goodness that exist in the space between them, they clink their glasses to this toast: "*Shabbat shalom.*" Rest and peace.

What would your life look like if you consistently reminded yourself that the world didn't revolve around you? What if you released all that concerned you and the functionality of your to-do list and just spent some time with the space between things? What if instead of gripping the world and working and hustling, you just let go and let God? How would it change you? How would it change those around you? What would it do for your family? Your friends? How would your stress level change if you turned off your phone and didn't answer e-mails for twenty-four hours once a week?

It might just be enough to remind you that you aren't a slave. It might be enough to convince you that the world is in God's hands and the weight of it too. It might release you to pay attention to the space between things instead of the things themselves. It might let freedom take root inside of you and work its way into the fabric of your everyday life. And if that's the case, then I salute you: *Shabbat shalom.*

Finding Freedom

What is keeping you from Sabbath rest?

How can you organize yourself to experience rest and peace on a regular basis?

CHAPTER 17

Staying Free

Do not deprive the foreigner or the
fatherless of justice, or take the cloak of
the widow as a pledge. Remember that
you were slaves in Egypt and the LORD
your God redeemed you from there.

DEUTERONOMY 24:17-18, NIV

I'M PART OF The Salvation Army. We wear uniforms with a big capital *S* on our lapels. Inside our movement there is an internal debate about whether the *S* stands for "saved to save" or "saved to serve." One time a very inebriated man stumbled into a shelter I was running and suggested they stood for "sexy soldier." I took it as a compliment.

I think it stands for "saved to save." William Booth, the cofounder of The Salvation Army, was always talking about the trajectory of freedom and equality in people's lives. He used to say that our job was to get people saved, keep them saved, and empower them to get someone else saved. In other words, the freedom of one person from oppression was the possibility of another person's freedom from oppression. Our freedom was for something greater than ourselves.

This is an important distinction. See, I grew up hearing that salvation was about saving me *from* things. And truly it is. But salvation is much bigger than that. Salvation not only frees me from things, it frees me *for* things.

When I first encountered the love of God, it loosened oppression's grip on my life. I began to see things differently. I desired adventure. I decided to replace my appetite for rebellion with mission, so I joined a group in Africa for a summer project. We built an orphanage in Malawi in the middle of a famine. It was life-changing. Up until that trip I had thought my salvation was about getting me free from addiction, crime, pain, and the trajectory of rebellion. And it was. But while I was on that trip, I accidently led someone else to Jesus.

In what I affectionately (and I think fairly accurately) describe as the worst gospel presentation in the history of the world, I presented this lovely girl Fatima with a tract of what it meant to follow Jesus. I did it because the mission group I was with made me do it. If I didn't do it, I would be in trouble and lose my free time, and I really didn't want to lose my free time, and I was sick and tired of being in trouble, so I did it. I went through this tract, and to my utmost surprise, Fatima wanted to follow Jesus. Trust me in this: I found this incredibly hard to believe. I made this poor girl sit through three presentations of the gospel tract just to make sure she heard it right.

After it was all done, I had a revelation. See, I had believed that God could save anyone. He had saved me! But what would change my life forever is that God could use me to save someone. That's what took me from saved (past tense) to save (present tense). I wasn't just saved from rebellion and loosened from oppression, I was saved *for* salvation; I was saved for freedom. I had a purpose and there was a plan.

This revelation and experience changed my whole life. Before slavery, before oppression, before all the mess of the Exodus, God wanted his people to represent him on the earth. He created them to care for the earth and model his character so that through them the entire world would be blessed. This is how Joseph got to Egypt before the beginning of the Exodus. He saved Egypt because he was saved to save and he knew it. Salvation was not just something he had and hung on to for himself. He shared it with everyone he could. Every place Joseph went was blessed because he shared his blessing with the people around him. From the house of Potiphar to his fellow prisoners to finally the Pharaoh himself. Joseph understood that he was saved to save.

A salvation that isn't shared is a denial of freedom. It's selfishness, and selfishness is the engine of oppression.

Years ago my friend was liberated from street prostitution. It's a long, beautiful story of oppression unraveling and grace flowing and heaven manifesting itself on earth. A story of salvation that is still so sweet it can make me cry. The week before Christmas she asked me if we could take our outreach van out on Christmas Day to visit her old friends, still stuck on the cold, hard streets of that northern Canadian city, still captives to the oppression of prostitution. I was delighted at the idea and asked if I could get some gifts ready to give them since it was Christmas. She beamed and said through a goofy grin, "I already bought them." That bitter, cold Christmas Day I witnessed freedom in its finest form as she handed out handpicked gifts with handwritten notes of love and hope to every woman we could find. It was not only evidence of someone whose life had been saved from oppression; it was the beauty of someone whose life had been saved for freedom.

Freedom is *for* something. It's an invitation to live another way. To demonstrate another kind of kingdom that is coming to the world. It's a freedom that says oppression will never have the last word.

If we believe freedom is only for ourselves, we are in danger of starting the cycle of oppression all over again. Contentment, denial, pride, fear, compromise, and it starts again. The cycle can only be permanently broken when we realize not only what we were saved *from* but what we are saved *for*.

On their journey to freedom, the Israelites had to keep their eyes and lives fixed on the Promised Land, and on living a new way. The laws that God passed through Moses were all about treating each other with fairness and justice. They are filled with economic equity and social justice—constant markers to move God's people to explore not just that they are free from Egypt; they are free for a purpose.

When you know that you are not only saved from something but for something, it frees you to get to the actual work of bringing God's Kingdom to the world. This journey will not be easy or quick. It will take a lot of time and effort and energy. But it will be worth it.

I remember visiting Australia and going to Bondi Beach in Sydney. Bondi Beach is famous for its surf, so I walked into a rental place on the beach and asked for a surfboard. Once they quizzed me and realized I only ever saw surfing in movies (I'm an avid fan of *Point Break* and *Blue Crush*), they relegated me to a boogie board and told me to stay between the flags. I was crushed. My hopes for surfing were dashed. But I wasn't destroyed; I still embarked on the boogie board of a lifetime.

By that I mean I almost died trying to bodysurf. After a few hours of being pummeled by the sheer power of the ocean and the riff of the waves, I took a break and talked to a real surfer on the shore.

I asked him the secret to good surfing. What he told me was more than information; it was revelation. He told me the secret to great surfing was working and waiting.

This is hard to swallow when you've been lured by the story of the wave. Surfers are in love with the wave—the moment when all the working and the waiting is culminated in this incredible force greater than themselves that they somehow harness and use to propel themselves into an anti-gravitational experience that suspends time. What happens when they catch a wave is "epic, dude." Have you ever watched it? It's magical.

But catching a wave takes work. And it involves waiting. Every time.

On the beach that day I realized something really important. Ministry is just like surfing.

The moment when God shows up is indescribable. Accidently leading Fatima to Jesus in Africa—the first time someone actually decided to follow Jesus after I told them the good news that it was possible—felt to me as though time were suspended and all of earth stood still and God descended and everything in me was completely and totally alive. And actually, that's kind of exactly what happens. See, the Scripture has two words for time: *chronos* and *kairos*. *Chronos* is a measurement of time in quantity. It's the time we keep. Our calendars mark off *chronos*, our clocks keep us in *chronos*, and our lives revolve around the seconds, minutes, hours, days, weeks, and years of *chronos*. We work and wait in *chronos*. *Chronos* ticks by inevitably.

Most of our lives are spent this way. Every hero, every reformer, every Bible character, every famous person who ever existed on the face of this time-trapped planet, spent most of their time in *chronos*. Working and waiting.

The Exodus story happened in *chronos*, real time. One commentator estimated that for the million and a half (at least) Israelites to cross the Red Sea, it would have taken close to a month. Working and waiting is quantity time. Seconds adding up to minutes adding up to hours and days and months and years of working and waiting. And for the Israelites, a lot of walking.

But then something happens. You know about this as much as I do. You've been working with someone for several years, and you figure you've missed the window for them to come to faith. Then they have a moment, a breakthrough. Maybe a blue bird in the sky poops on their head, and as they're scraping off the sticky white stuff, everything you've been depositing in them drops into place and they just get it! Revelation! In a spiritual sense, they are saved, delivered, and committed in one big moment. Time was suspended, and something magical happened.

This is called *kairos*. This is the kind of time God works in—time that is measured in quality, not quantity. It's "the time of your life." No one ever asks how long the time of your life lasts; it's a matter of quality, not quantity.

Kairos is why God is always present, why *now* is the time, and *today* is the day, of salvation. God is always measuring time differently than we do—where we are trapped (on this side of eternity) in *chronos*, he is *kairos*.

If we are real surfers—not wannabes but people willing to put in the time working and waiting—we will be attentive to both kinds of time. God is in both *kairos* and *chronos*, and so are we. Like the Israelites, our journey is not just a nice moment but a whole new way of life, a long walk.

You never hear surfers or preachers talk much about the working and waiting. We love the *kairos* stuff. But the truth of the matter is that most of life is lived in *chronos*.

Over the past year the Lord began to challenge me to talk more about the working and the waiting. I'm meant to remind you of the moments between *kairos* moments, when God's people crossed deserts, waited in prison, were shipwrecked, beaten, beheaded, and lost. I'm talking more about the *chronos* moments when I'm bored stiff of preaching one more time, taking another flight, leaving my kids, or talking on the phone with yet another desperate person in crisis while I'm with my own family at the park. I want to tell you about the hours and hours and hours I spend praying, locked in a prayer room so I can't escape the boring inevitability of my own pathetic doubts and fears and requests. I want to tell you about the endless seemingly circular conversations I have with the same people about the same issues over and over and over again.

Sometimes I'm tempted to think I made up the wave. Sometimes I think the waiting and working are never going to end. But then, in the nick of time—the fullness of time—a *kairos* moment interrupts the humdrum of my own *chronos*, and I'm up and surfing the wave. Epic indeed.

If you read the Exodus story with this idea in mind, you will see it everywhere. The walking, the waiting, the assembly of the tent, the lineup for Moses' advice on daily matters—the inertia. Life in real time. And then *kairos* comes, and everything becomes clear. An epic moment punctuates the monotonous reality. All of the journey is worth it.

You can't have the wave until you do the time. If you can't swim, can't wait, can't balance, then you can't surf. When the wave comes, you'll be tossed and spit out on the shore. Surfing is more than a funky haircut, some funky slang, and a cool wardrobe. It's not for posers. So is being the people of God on the earth. It's for people who are committed to the work, who love the wave enough to train and spend time positioning themselves in the right places at just the right moments.

I've met too many people who watch others surf and think it's easy. When they try it out, they find themselves like me on a boogie board on Bondi Beach. They are beaten by the exhausting reality of just trying to break the surf. Seriously.

And this is when it hit me. Real surfers love *all the time* in the ocean. Once you break yourself in and learn to swim and paddle and hang out on the board, once you sense the rhythm and learn to read the signs and signals of the ocean, real surfers love it *all*. They forget that it's waiting and work. They love the whole thing.

God is looking for people who love the whole thing.

God is not just in the *kairos* moment. He's in every single moment. He's in the waiting and the working. He's using every single event and thing in your life to work his purposes out in your life. He is growing your faith, stretching your perseverance, infusing you with hope, uplifting you with joy. He is training and using and surfing with you.

Following God is often hard work. You have to spend a lot of time swimming against the current. When you are in that moment when you think the Bible study at your place where only three people showed up is a failure and that the whole night was a waste of time. When you are telling some-one about your newfound freedom and even you wish you could just stop speaking because it doesn't seem to be work-ing. When the regret of not doing it right rings in your head for days. When you wonder why you are spending two nights a week volunteering with people when you can't even find time to go on a date with your spouse. All of those moments and people you think are a waste of your time—they are part of the ocean. They are part of the ultimate epic pattern of God. It's God's Kingdom coming to earth. All of it.

So, I'm back in training to surf Kingdom style.

- I'm committed to being a real follower of God—not a poser. It's not about the haircut or the lingo. It's not about the image or the hype. It's about the substance. Can I swim? Can I paddle? Can I go the distance, against the current?

- I will put in the practice. I will not despise the small beginnings. I will not be discouraged by crashing and falling. I will get back on my board and try again. I will use every opportunity to grow the substance of faith required for every *kairos* moment.

- I will be disciplined. This will require me waking up early to pray. To actually read God's Word for what he wants to say to me. To study and learn and engage in culture. I've got to have the physique to match the challenge.

- I will speak often about the wave. I will watch others surf—with longing and desire, yes, but also with awe and fear. I will listen and hear the *kairos* stories of others with joy because every time God shows up for anyone is evidence that he will show up for me, too. I will help others to fall in love with God by talking about his amazing power and the revelation of his love.

- I will try and not stop trying. I will knock on doors and show up at homes and street corners and feel like a dork all over again as I speak to people who look way too cool for me. I will fall and not stop falling if it means that one time I might be able to stand and surf for a while. I will crash and almost drown if necessary to learn to stand up and ride the wave.

- I will enjoy the ocean. I will choose to see time from God's perspective. I will commit to enjoying the journey—to consider it pure joy, even in the trials, to be present in the plan of salvation God has for the earth.

- I will spend the time. All the time I can will be spent in the ocean. Practicing, hanging, waiting, balancing, learning, trying, swimming—working and waiting.

- I will remind myself that surfing cannot be learned through a book, a website, an article, or a movie. There is only one way to learn to surf: You have to get in the ocean. I'm going to minister. Evangelize. Pray. Serve. Sabbath. Give. Believe. By *doing it,* not talking about doing it, reading about doing it, listening to someone else doing it, berating myself for not doing it. I'm going to just get out and do it.

- I'm going to learn to surf when *no one is watching*. This is not about what people think of me, or what will get me the most positive feedback or best gig. This is about me and the ocean. This is a private battle. When I get really good, I won't care who is watching anymore. I'll be lost in the ocean—captured by the wave.

- I'll be proud to be called a surfer. I'll identify completely with the calling of God on my life. I won't apologize for not being like others or living a different way. I'll stop thinking I'm doing something wrong when I'm tired and sore. I will embrace what God has called and invited me to. This will be my joy.

The beginning and ending of the Exodus story are relatively fluid. Does the story begin with Moses in front of Pharaoh? In front of the burning bush? Floating in a basket down the Nile? Does it start with midwives daring to defy an untenable command or a prisoner daring to interpret the dream of the king? Does it end when the Israelites step out of Egypt or step into the Promised Land? Like I say, it's fluid. But there's an undeniably big moment in the middle, when the people of God take a deep, collective breath and step out into a raging body of water. It's just another step in the passage of *chronos* time—until suddenly the waters part, and they find themselves surfing through *kairos* time. God is there. God is with them. They are free. Living not just a memory of a freedom moment, but living out the ultimate freedom—slaves no longer.

Finding Freedom

Can you make the commitments listed here?

Who can join you in this invitation to waiting and working, trusting that God is with you and will lead you into the *kairos* moments he's preparing you for?

Acknowledgments

CLAUDIO OLIVER, who got me started on asking all the right questions about the Exodus;

David Zimmerman, who is a gracious, kind, and amazing editor;

Joyce Ellery, who refused to give up on freedom for my life;

The Salvation Army, for starting a trajectory of freedom in my family's genealogy;

Kristine, who always tells me the truth;

Stephen Court, who spurs me on;

Amy and Stacy, for being my Infinitum partners;

Doreen, for helping free me to write;

And so many others whose lives have impacted me and who continue to fight in *chronos* for freedom to come for real life.